Adobe® PHOTOSHOP CS2

ONE-CLICK WOW!

Over 900 Incredible
One-Click Style Makeovers,
Brushes, Tool Presets, Patterns,
Shapes, Actions & Rollovers—
All on CD—To Instantly Enhance
Your Photos, Graphics & Type

Jack Davis

Adobe Photoshop CS2 One-Click Wow!
Jack Davis

Peachpit Press
1249 Eighth Street
Berkeley, CA 94710
(510) 524-2178
(510) 524-2221 (fax)

Find us on the Web at www.peachpit.com

Peachpit Press is a division of Pearson Education

Adobe Photoshop CS2 One-Click Wow! is published in association with Adobe Press

To report errors, please send a note to errata@peachpit.com

Copyright © 2006 by Jack Davis and Linnea Dayton
Cover design: Jack Davis
Book design: Jill Davis
Production and prepress: Jill Davis
Direct-to-plate printing: Quebecor World / Taunton, Massachusetts

ISBN 0-321-24644-6

0 9 8 7 6 5 4 3 2 1

Printed and bound in the United States of America

To Him from whom all blessings flow...

— Jack

ACKNOWLEDGMENTS
As always, I had a great deal of help with putting this book and CD-ROM together. First, I personally want to acknowledge Linnea Dayton, my partner of over 10 years. Though she was not involved in this specific version of *One-Click Wow!* her expertise is evident throughout, due to her work on previous editions. I also want to thank the friends and family of both Linnea and myself who let us "style" some of their photos to help illustrate the pages. And my thanks go to Piper Carr and others at Corbis Images who allowed us to use photos from their Royalty Free collections when my own just wouldn't fill the bill.

Several people helped make sure this CD-and-book package communicates clearly. I am especially grateful to my wonderful wife and partner Jill Davis for designing and producing this (and many other Wow editions) book!

I'd also like to thank the many supporters at Peachpit Press—in particular, my publisher Nancy Ruenzel, editor Rebecca Gulick, production coodinator David Van Ness, and media producers Victor Gavenda and Jay Payne, who did invaluable and extensive manuscript/CD testing.

Finally, thanks to all who have helped with nine editions of *The Photoshop Wow! Book.* The experience that was gained in that project has made *Adobe Photoshop CS2 One-Click Wow!* possible, and I'm delighted to pass it on.

CONTENTS

How To Use This Book & CD-ROM   1
Read the book for "how-to" pointers and
inspirational examples for using all the
One-Click Wow! Presets on the CD-ROM.

One-Click Wow! Quick Start   3
Can't wait to get started? Here's how to get up
and running right away.

Sample Gallery   6
Here, to inspire you, are some examples of
One-Click Wow! Styles applied to a range
of photos.

1 USING ONE-CLICK WOW! STYLES   12

What Is a Layer Style?   13
A Layer Style is a way to enhance a photo, type,
or graphics — instantly! — by "overlaying"
color texture, dimension, framing, etc.

Dynamic Wow Button Rollover Styles   14

Layer Style "Magic"   15
After you apply a Style, you can continue to
make changes to the layer or to the Style itself.

Scaling a Style   16
Customizing Styles   18
Copying and Pasting Styles   20
Using Styles with Layer & Clipping Masks   21
Working with Styles in ImageReady   23

Saving, Sizing & Output   24
Here's how to choose a file format for your
"styled" file and how to resize the file if needed.

A Layer Style Tutorial   28
This step-by-step tutorial walks you through a
sample project, showing you how to apply Layer
Styles, change layer content while keeping the
Style, copy a Style, and how to scale a Style.

2: STYLES FOR PHOTOS — 33

Photo Gallery — 34

Photo Effects Samples — 38

Use this "catalog" to choose Styles for your photos or digital paintings.

Edges — 38

Frames — 40

Tints & Antique Effects — 42

Color Overlay Effects — 44

Darkroom & Image-Enhancing Effects — 46

Film Grain, Noise & Mezzotints — 48

Paper, Canvas & Other Texture Overlays — 50

3: STYLES FOR TYPE & GRAPHICS — 52

Type & Graphics Gallery — 53

These pages offer examples of **One-Click Wow! Styles** applied to type, clip art, and custom graphics.

Graphics & Type Effects Samples — 58

Use this "catalog" to choose Styles that will turn your type and graphics into objects you'll want to reach out and touch!

Chromes — 58

Metals — 60

Glass, Ice & Crystal — 62

Gems & Smooth Stones — 64

Plastics — 66

Polished & Textured Woods — 68

Rock, Brick & Other Materials — 70

Organic Patterns — 72

Patterns & Fabrics — 74

Strokes & Fills — 76

Shadows, Halos & Embossing — 78

Glows & Neons — 80

Button Rollover Styles — 82

4: OTHER WOW! PRESETS   84

How to Use the Wow! Custom Shape Overlays   85

Overlay Shapes & Styles Gallery   86

Text Panel Overlay Variations   88

Oval Frame Variations   90

Brush Frame Variations   92

How To Paint with the Wow! Paint & Clone Presets   93

Brush Stroke Borders   96

Painting Gallery   98
Here are some examples of the stunning variety of traditional-media effects you can get with the **Wow! Media Brush Presets** to turn photos into paintings.

Pattern Stamp & Art History Presets   100
These sample paintings, made from the same original (or source) photo, demonstrate how you can combine your work with the **Wow! Media Brush Presets** with the **Wow-Texture Styles**.

Patterns Sampler   102
Here are samples from the 6 different libraries of **Wow Pattern Presets** (which are also integrated into many of the Wow Styles)

Using the Wow! Image Fix Brushes   104

Using the Wow! Actions   105

Wow! Actions   106

Gradient Effects   108
These **Gradient Presets** can also be useful for filling type or graphics, or for designing backgrounds.

How To Use This Book & CD-ROM

The book tells how to apply and customize the hundreds of One-Click Wow! Presets on the CD-ROM.

▶ *Throughout the book are tips in this format—starting with an orange pointer to catch your eye. The tips provide useful information about working with the One-Click Wow Presets in Photoshop. Here are some tips you may find especially useful:*

- *Converting a Background to a layer that can accept Styles (page 4)*
- *Understanding the relationship between the One-Click Wow! Styles and your file's Resolution setting (page 16)*
- *Controlling brush tip size with keyboard shortcuts (page 94)*
- *Choosing a file format for saving your finished image (page 26)*

Here's what you'll find on the ***Adobe Photoshop One-Click Wow!*** CD-ROM:

- **More than 300 sophisticated Layer Styles** for enhancing your photos, type, and artwork (in the **Wow-Styles** folder)
- **Another 150 Styles, especially for buttons,** plus **50 combined Rollover Styles** for automatic interactivity (in the **Wow-20 Button Styles.asl** file, also in the **Wow-Styles** folder)
- **Wow-Styles Tutorial.psd files** for practicing all aspects of working with Styles (in the **Wow-Styles Tutorial** folder)
- **Wow Tool Presets** that imitate traditional art media such as watercolor, oils, and chalk. Some of these Presets are designed for "cloning" a source image as a painting using Photoshop's **Pattern Stamp** and **Art History Brush** tools. Others are designed for painting from scratch with the **Brush** tool.

*Here the **Wow-Custom Shape Overlay Presets,** specifically the **Wow-Frame-Oval-Ghosted White** (left) and the **Wow-Frame-Brush-Ghosted Black** (right). Create elaborate framing effects with one simple click-and-drag.*

- Other **Wow Tool Presets** include the new **Wow-Custom Shape Overlays** for sophisticated framing and panel effects (see page 85 for more on these new One-Click

wonders!) and the **Wow-Image Fix Presets** for using the Brush tool to lighten and darken specific areas of an image, to whiten teeth and eyes, and to neutralize redness on the skin.

- **More than 75 Wow Actions** that give you quick, automated options for creating special effects and carrying out production tasks. A few of the complex dimensional effects you'll find for type and graphics are brushed metal, crystal, and fire. Effects for photos include soft focus, blurred background, watercolor, line work, stippling,

With the Actions palette in Button Mode, the Wow Actions appear in color-coded sets.

mezzotint, bordering, and colorizing. Automated production tasks include tone and color corrections and others. Try them out on the files in the **Wow-Actions Testers** folder.

- **40 Gradient Presets** (in the **Wow-Gradients** folder) that you can use in your own Styles, in Gradient Fill layers, or with the Gradient tool to make backgrounds or multicolor tints.
- **More than 150 seamlessly tiling Pattern Presets** (in the **Wow-Patterns** folder) that can be used as fills and Fill layers or as Strokes, Overlays, or Textures in customizing or creating Layer Styles.

*Once installed, the **Wow-Patterns Presets** are available to any Photoshop dialog box or palette that uses Patterns.*

▶ *The "see also" eye* 👁 *points out related sections of the book, in case you need more information. For instance:* 👁 *See "Scaling a Style" on pages 16–17 to learn about the important relationship between Layer Styles and the Resolution setting.*

▶ *You can use a Wow Style to "harmonize" a series of photos.*

*Here the **Wow-Tint FX 11** Style not only created a romantic mood, but also overcame differences in color and tone to instantly unify this wedding collage.*

I n this ***Adobe Photoshop One-Click Wow!*** book you'll find these sections that show you how to use the contents of the CD:

• Turn to "**One-Click Wow! Quick Start**" on pages 3–4 to learn how to install the **Wow-Styles** and other **Wow Presets**, and how to apply a Style.

• "**Layer Style 'Magic,'**" starting on page 15, begins by demonstrating how flexible and easy to use Styles are. Also included in "Layer Style 'Magic'" are tips for "**Scaling a Style**" once you've applied it (pages 16–17); "**Customizing Styles**" so you can modify them and then easily apply them again later (pages 18–19), "**Copying & Pasting Styles**" to apply the same Style to other photos, type, or graphics (page 20); "**Using Styles with Layer & Clipping Masks**" for styling images "framed" within a shape or type (pages 21–22), and

*You can customize any **Wow Style** by applying it and then making changes in the Layer Styles dialog box. Here the Size setting for Bevel And Emboss was scaled up from its original 7 pixels (left) to 70 pixels, to change the "carving" without changing the wood grain, lighting, or Shadow.*

"**Working with Styles in ImageReady**" (page 23).

• "**Saving, Sizing & Output**" (pages 24–27) shows how to make a file the right size and format for printing, posting on the Web, or attaching to an email.

• "**A Layer Style Tutorial**" (pages 28–32)

walks you step-by-step through working with Styles in Photoshop and ImageReady. The **Wow-Styles Tutorial** files needed for working along with the steps are provided on the CD-ROM.

• Pages 33–83 include "**Gallery**" sections to inspire you, as well as printed samples of the Layer Styles provided on the CD. These examples are organized in two sections—"**Styles for Photos**" (pages 34–51) and "**Styles for Type & Graphics**" (pages 52–83), including "**Button Rollover Styles**" (on page 82).

• Page 84 introduces the four kinds of Wow Presets other than Styles, with tips for using the **Wow–Crop and Marquee Presets** and the **Wow-Pattern Presets**.

• "**How To Paint with the Wow! Paint & Clone Presets**" (on pages 93–95) tells how to work with the **Wow-Pattern Stamp, Art History,** and **Art Media Presets,** with suggestions for when to choose each of these three matched sets of artists' tools. The "**Painting Gallery**" and "**Pattern Stamp and Art History Presets**" (pages 98–101) show the results you can get by combining the cloning Presets with matching **Wow Patterns** (shown on pages 102–103).

• "**Using the Wow! Image Fix Brushes**" (page 104) not only shows how to use these retouching brushes, but also suggests how to improve the overall tone, color, and condition of your photos before you begin the retouching process.

• "**Using the Wow! Actions**" (page 105) and the Actions samples that follow it (pages 106–107) provide instructions and examples for these "try 'em, you'll like 'em" routines.

• "**Gradient Effects**" (pages 108–109) is a "catalog" of the **Wow-Gradient Presets**.

One-Click Wow! Quick Start

Can't wait to get started? Here's how to get going right away.

▶ Note: if you use Image-Ready, you may want to *move the Wow Styles (found within the One-Click Wow Presets folder you just copied into Photoshop's Presets folder) into the Styles folder, within Photoshop's Presets folder. This will make them available to both Photoshop and Image-Ready. If you don't use Image-Ready, forget I mentioned it.*

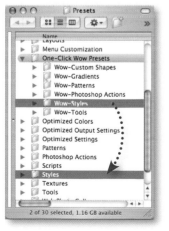

To install and use the **One-Click Wow! Layer Styles** and other Presets, you'll need to **first install Adobe Photoshop.** Then follow the numbered steps below.

1 Installing the One-Click Wow! Styles and other Presets. Insert the **One-Click Wow! CD-ROM** into your computer's CD-ROM drive **and double-click its icon**, or use My Computer (Windows); locate and **copy the One-Click Wow Presets folder from this book's CD into Photoshop's Presets folder.**

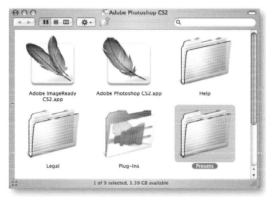

Photoshop's Presets folder is in the Adobe Photoshop application folder.

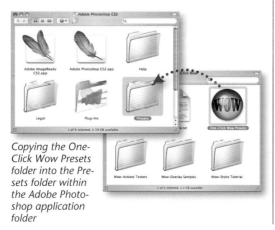

Copying the One-Click Wow Presets folder into the Presets folder within the Adobe Photoshop application folder

2 Starting up the Adobe Photoshop program. If Photoshop is already running, you'll need to quit the program and start it again so it can "find" the **Wow Styles** and other Presets that you've copied to Photoshop's Presets folders.

For convenience in working with Styles, be sure to have both the Layers palette and the Styles palette open. To open the Layers palette, **choose Window > Layers.** Open the Styles palette the same way (**choose Window > Styles**).

So that you can see the full names of the Styles, along with thumbnails large enough to see what the Styles look like, click the **little triangle in the upper-right corner of the Styles palette and choose Large List from the pop-out menu.**

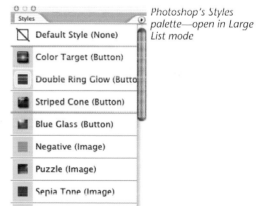

Photoshop's Styles palette—open in Large List mode

3 Preparing the file for working with One-Click Wow! Styles. Now open a file that you want to "style" (**choose File > Open**). You can duplicate the file for safe-keeping if you like.

So that you'll get good results right away when you apply a **Wow Style** to the file, change the Resolution setting for the file as

▶ *If you try to apply a Style to a Background layer, nothing will happen. To convert a Background to a non-Background layer so that a Style can be applied, double-click the "Background" name in the Layers palette; then in the New Layer dialog box, click OK.*

First double-click here.

Then click here.

follows: **Choose Image > Image Size**; in the Image Size dialog box, **make sure the "Resample Image" option is OFF** (no check mark in the box). **Then double-click to select the number in the Resolution setting box, type in 225; click OK.**

Changing the Resolution setting to 225 pixels/inch

4 Applying a Style. To target the layer where you want to apply a **One-Click Wow! Style, click the layer's name in the Layers palette.** (As the tip at the left explains, you can't apply a Style to the *Background*.)

The layer is targeted and ready for a Style to be applied.

To apply one of the **One-Click Wow! Styles** to the targeted layer, first **click the triangle in the upper-right corner of the Styles palette and choose the library of Styles you want from the list at the bottom of the pop-out menu.** (To get a good look at the contents of each library so you can decide

which one to choose, check the examples on pages 32–45 and 52–75 of this book.)

*Choosing the **Wow-01 Edge Styles** set*

In the caution box that appears, for now it's safest to click Append, so that you don't accidentally delete any Styles that may currently be in the Styles palette but haven't yet been saved as part of a Styles library. ◉ *See the tip on page 5 for an explanation of when to append Styles to the palette and when to replace the current Styles.*

Append adds the Styles library you chose to the current list; "OK" replaces the current Styles.

With the **Wow-01 Edge Styles** loaded into the Styles palette, click the particular Style you want to apply.

*Choosing the **Wow-Edges 08** Style*

One-Click Wow! Quick Start

continued

▶ *Although both Photoshop and ImageReady have Styles palettes, appending or replacing Styles in one program's palette doesn't affect the Styles palette in the other program. Each program's Styles palette has to be "stocked" with Styles separately.*

▶ *Photoshop and its Web-design companion Image-Ready are equipped with little context-sensitive labels called "Tool Tips." In either program if you pause the cursor over some part of the interface, a Tool Tip will pop up to identify the item under the cursor. You can turn the Tool Tips function on or off by choosing Edit > Preferences > General and clicking in the "Show Tool Tips" box.*

👁 *See "Working with Styles in ImageReady" on page 23 and step 10 of "A Layer Style Tutorial" on page 32 for pointers on using Styles in ImageReady.*

The Style will be applied to your file instantly! You'll see the result in the working window, and in the Layers palette an 𝑓 icon appears next to the layer name.

The Wow-Edges 08 Style applied

👁 **See pages 12–27 for pointers on working with Styles in Photoshop, and pages 28–32 for a step-by-step tutorial.**

Getting started with Styles in Image-Ready. To work with Styles in ImageReady (Photoshop's companion Web-design program), start up the program from the desk-top or by clicking the "Jump to ImageReady" button at the very bottom of Photoshop's Tools palette. Once ImageReady is open, any Styles libraries you've loaded into Photoshop's Styles folder (described in step 1 on page 3) will also be available to Image-Ready's Styles palette.

To begin working with Styles, be sure the Layers palette and Styles palette are open (**Window > Layers** and **Window > Styles**). To see the name and thumbnail for each Style in the palette, **click the little triangle** near the top-right corner of the palette and **choose Small List**.

The **Wow-20 Button Styles** library was designed especially for use with ImageReady. To load this library, choose it from the Styles palette's pop-out menu. To apply a particular **Wow-Button Style, click the target layer's name** in the Layers palette, then **click on a Wow Style** in the Styles palette.

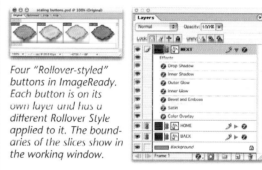

In ImageReady's Styles palette, even in the tiny thumbnails of Small List mode, you can see a black triangle in the upper-left corner of each Rollover Style. A Rollover Style makes on-screen buttons change in response to what the user does.

As in Photoshop, the Style will be applied to your file instantly, and the 𝑓 icon will appear next to the layer's name in the Layers palette. If the Style you've applied is a Roll-over, the slice icon 🔪 will also appear, between the layer's name and the 𝑓, to show that the Rollover Style has automatically created a rectangular area that will respond when the cursor enters or leaves it.

Four "Rollover-styled" buttons in ImageReady. Each button is on its own layer and has a different Rollover Style applied to it. The boundaries of the slices show in the working window.

To see a "Rollover-styled" button in action after you've applied the Style, click the Pre-view Document tool near the bottom of the Tools palette to put the file into Preview mode. Then move the cursor into the slice to see the Over state and click to see the Down state.

Click on the Preview Document tool to test the Rollover Style you've applied.

Samples Gallery

Here are just a few samples of what you can do with the 21 different libraries that make up the **One-Click Wow Styles.** As you can see, all the Layer Styles conform to whatever shape is on the particular layer that they are applied to—whether that is a photograph or a graphic. For some of the images shown here, the Styles have been scaled to fit the specific subject. 👁 *See "Scaling a Style" on page 16 for tips on scaling.*

1 *Frame 02*, and **6** *Frame 04,* are wooden frames with mats. **2** *Frame 08* is a woven frame that has been scaled here 200%. **3** *Gems 13* turns type into an abalone shell sculpture under resin. **4** *Like all styles, Halo 06's* grainy light and dark edges conform to the shape of the content of the layer. **5** *Tint FX 04* is a sepiatone treatment with an inner glow and outer shadow. **7** *Plastic 09* is a transparent blue/green color. **8** *Metals 04* imitates hand beaten gold. **9** *Edges 07* "coats" anything on the layer with glossy plastic. **10** *Halo 08* is a rounded emboss. **11** *Metals 01* is rusted and pitted, and **12** *Frame 10* has a floral pattern and matching mat.

continued on page 8

6

7

8

9

10

11

12

Samples Gallery
continued

1 *An overlaid canvas texture is added to* **Tint FX 09**'s *brown duotone effect and inner glow and drop shadow.* **2 Stroke 09** *has a grainy burgundy inner glow, a mustard-colored outer stroke and a hard-edged drop shadow.* **3 Chrome 02** *is brightly lit with subtle reflections.* **4 Halo 01** *has intense white and black inner and outer halos, as well as edging effects.* **5 Tint FX 09** *applies a brown tint but keeps some of the original color.* **6 Darkroom 14** *subtly lightens the center of a photo while darkening the edges (try* **Darkroom 01, 03, and 11–15** *for similar subtle enhancements).* **7 Texture 02** *adds a canvas texture overlay to any image or digital painting.* **8 Darkroom 07** *"posterizes" a photo, with results based on the image's colors (try* **Color FX 07** *for a similar effect).* **9 Metals 19** *is a chiseled polished steel which works great for graphics or type with lots of complex detail.* **10 Edges 01** *adds a dark inner halo to a photo, while* **11 Glass 03** *is a "chipped" polished glass effect.* **12 Edges 03** *adds a bright halo.* **13 Organics 05** *adds a dimensional stroke and a woven mat interior to text or graphics.*

continued on page 10

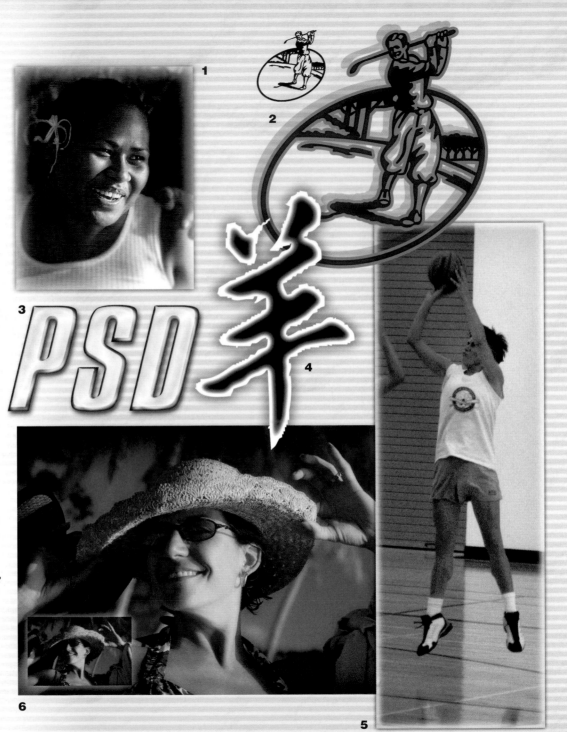

Samples Gallery

continued

1 Organics 11 *is a recycled paper fill with beveled edges.*
2 Chrome 06 *adds a dark, reflective dimensionality.*
3 Frame 05 *is a hardwood (the Style has been scaled here 200% to better fit the photo. See page 16 for more on Scaling Styles).* **4 Stroke 15** *adds a bright red fill, a brown stroke and a dark halo (also scaled here to better fit the graphic).* **5 Darkroom 08** *adds drama to clouds and sunsets by overlaying a multicolored gradient (especially good for when the horizon is in the lower third of the photo).* **6 Stroke 11**'s *grainy purple inner glow and golden stroke also works great with black on transparent clip art.*
7 Edges 09 *inverts the color of an image at the edges.* **8 Tint FX 01**'s *partial sepia overlay can give a quick hand-tinted effect.* **9 Stroke 03** *is a simple white fill and black stroke and shadow.* **10 Organics 13**'s *fill is a multicolored rust.* **11 Rock 18** *turns anything into polished, chiseled granite, while* **12 Halo 12** *is perfect for turning your logo into a subtle "watermark."*
13 Metals 16 *is glowing antique gold.* **14 Frame 09**'s *glass edges follow the contour of any piece of clip art.* **15 Tint FX 07** *adds a blue color overlay with halos and* **16 Gems 07** *instantly turns a piece of type or graphic into a granite countertop.*

Southwestern Style

1 Using One-Click Wow! Styles

The next 20 pages show how to work with the **One-Click Wow! Styles** to transform your Photoshop projects from "ho-hum" to "Wow!" instantly. Whether you start with type, graphics, photos, or Photoshop paintings like those shown in Section 4 of this book, you can achieve professional results with just one click in the Styles palette.

You'll also learn how to scale a Style, if necessary, to fit your particular project, and how to work with Styles (including Rollovers) in ImageReady. Any **Wow Style** can be used as a starting point for developing more Styles of your own, either in Photoshop or in ImageReady, by changing one or more component effects to taste and then saving the new Style so you can use it again. A quick "Layer Style Tutorial" starting on page 28 will lead you step-by-step through applying, customizing, and saving Styles.

To make sure you get the best-looking output possible, you'll find a section (pages 24–27) on how to prepare Photoshop files for successful output, either in print or on the Web.

▶ *One-Click Wow! Styles can be applied to files of any resolution, but they are easiest to work with in files whose Resolution setting is 225 pixels/inch.* ◉ *See the tip on page 17 for more.*

What Is a Layer Style?

Use Styles to instantly (!) improve photos, type, or graphics by "overlaying" color, texture, dimension, framing or any of a dozen other effects.

▶ *A separate book-and-CD-ROM package—**Adobe Photoshop Elements One-Click Wow!**—has Styles and instructions specifically adapted for Adobe Photoshop Elements.*

Simply stated, a Layer Style is a "look" that you can add to photos, type, or graphics *instantly*—simply by clicking in the Styles palette. Below are a few of the highly sophisticated kinds of effects you can apply with the Styles from the **One-Click Wow! CD-ROM**. To create such a treatment *without* using Layer Styles could take a lot of time, work, and skill, as shown at the right.

*A Style can be a color treatment such as a "partial sepiatone" (**Wow-Tint FX 01**) or an exaggeration of color and contrast (**Wow-Darkroom 04**).*

*A Style can provide edge effects for photos, such as a modern border treatment (**Wow-Edges 05**) or an antique wooden frame (**Wow-Frame 05**).*

*A Style can turn plain type or graphics into convincing material objects, such as chiseled steel (**Wow-Metals 17**) or transparent blue plastic (**Wow-Plastic 08**).*

At the Wow! intergalactic headquarters, we've used the following "ingredients" to cook up the **One-Click Wow! Layer Styles**:

- A **drop shadow**, sharp or soft
- An **inner shadow** that extends inward from the edge of the artwork, which can produce a "carved" effect
- Light or dark **glows** that extend inward or outward from the edges of the art
- A **beveled edge**, wide or narrow, sharp or rounded
- An **overlay** of a single color, a gradient, or a pattern that changes or even replaces the original color of a photo, type, or graphic
- An **opacity** control that can make the "styled" artwork partly or fully transparent
- A **texture** that creates bumps and pits on the surface of the artwork
- A **stroke**—even a multicolor stroke—that outlines the edges of the art
- A "**satin**" treatment that can add sophisticated reflection and refraction effects

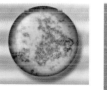

*With a Layer Style (**Wow-Gems 02**), you can turn a solid gray circle into the gemstone lozenge above. Or you can achieve the same result without a Style, by building the 11-layer file at the right, with the original circle serving as the base of a clipping group. The choice is a "no-brainer"!*

Bevel shadow
Bevel highlight
Inner shadow
Inner glow
"Satin" effect
Color overlay
Pattern overlay
Original gray circle
Outer glow
Drop shadow
Background

Dynamic Wow Button Rollover Styles

▶ *Each of the One-Click Wow! Rollover Styles has built-in JavaScript code that changes the look of the buttons in response to the cursor. If you're curious about the code, you can click the "Preview in Default Browser" button at the bottom of ImageReady's Tools palette and read it.*

In ImageReady, Styles can be used in all the same ways they can be used in Photoshop. But in addition, ImageReady can use *Rollover Styles,* which provide the "on-screen activity" for buttons on Web pages and other interactive interfaces. These Rollovers provide the color, dimension, and JavaScript programming that make on-screen buttons change, depending on what the user is doing. The **Wow Button** Styles that have the words "All Three" in their names are Rollover Styles. Found in the **Wow-20 Button Styles** library, they have three states:

*The **Normal** state is the way the button looks as it sits and waits for a Web site visitor to interact with it.*

*When the site visitor moves the cursor over the button, the **Over** state brings the button to life. The change from Normal to Over is designed to catch the eye, signaling that clicking the button will make something happen.*

*When the visitor clicks the button, the **Down** state appears, signaling that the click has been noted and something will now happen.*

The **Wow Button-All Three** Styles provide a wide range of options for the Normal state, as shown in the examples below on the left. The Over state often lights up the button or changes its color. And the Down state typically makes the button look "pushed," closer to the surface it sits on, or even depressed slightly below the surface.

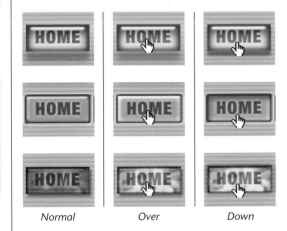

Normal   Over   Down

Layer Style "Magic"

After you apply a Style, it's easy to make changes to the layer content or to the Style itself.

► To remove a Layer Style from a layer, you can right-click (Windows) or Ctrl-click (Mac) the ℗ icon next to the layer's name in the Layers palette to open a context-sensitive menu, where you can **choose Clear Layer Style**. Or click the "Clear Style" button at the bottom of the Styles palette:

L ayer Styles are extremely flexible! Once you've applied a Style, **you can change the content of the layer and the Layer Style will conform to the changes.**

*If you apply a Style (here **Wow-Metals 06**) to a type layer and then change the font, the Style is retained.*

You can even edit the text, and the Style will conform to the new wording.

*If you reshape your graphics, the Style (here **Wow-Metals 19** with its beveled edge and highlighting) conforms to the new shape.*

*If you paint or draw on a layer that already has a Style applied to it, the Style (here **Wow-Plastic 07**) will automatically be added to each new stroke as you create it.*

N ot only can you change the content of a "styled" layer (as shown in the examples at the left), but **you can also completely replace the Style or change its individual attributes.**

*Here the **Wow-Chrome 10** Style was applied (bottom) completely replacing **Wow-Metals 06**.*

I n ImageReady, Rollover Styles and the layer-based slices associated with them also conform to the shape of the layer content, **so you can transform a button's shape and still retain the Style,** including the rollover interactivity.

*The **Wow Button 03-All Three** Rollover Style was applied to four identical buttons on four different layers. Shown here is the Normal state, with the bounding boxes for the interactive slices.*

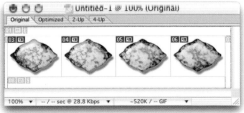

When the button graphics were stretched, the Style conformed to the new shape, and the slices were automatically redrawn to fit.

Scaling a Style

To "custom-fit" a Layer Style to a particular file, try scaling the Style.

▶ *Each Layer Style "remembers" the Resolution setting of the Photoshop file in which it was created. The **One-Click Wow! Styles** were created in files with a Resolution setting of 225 pixels/inch. Although these Styles can be applied to files of any resolution, they are easiest to work with if you first make sure the Resolution setting for your file is 225 pixels/inch. You can do this —without altering your image at all—by choosing **Image > Image Size**, then making sure "Resample Image" is turned OFF, and typing in "225" for the Resolution setting, as explained in step 3 of "One-Click Wow! Quick Start" on pages 3–5.*

After you apply a Layer Style, there's a good chance you'll want to scale it. That's because a Style can look different depending on whether you apply it to a thick or thin graphic, a bold or lightweight typeface, or a large or small photo.

1 Apply the Style. The first step is to **apply a Layer Style** as described in "One-Click Wow! Quick Start" on pages 3–5 or in "Copying & Pasting Styles" on page 20.

Great Grandma's portrait needs a frame.

*But the frame and mat applied by the **Wow-Frame 03** Style (page 10) seem to cover up too much of the photo. The Style needs to be scaled.*

2 Scaling. Right-click (Windows) or Ctrl-click (Mac) on the *f* icon to the right of the styled layer's name in the Layers palette, and **choose Scale Effects from the context-sensitive menu that pops out.** In the Scale Layer Effects dialog box, to pop out the Scale slider, **click the little triangle** to the left of

the "%" sign. **Move the slider** until the Layer Style looks right. Or type in a specific percentage, according to the suggestions in the **Note** below.

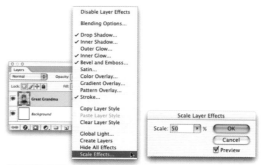

Using the context-sensitive menu to open the Scale Layer Effects dialog box (above left) and scaling the Style to 50% (above) improves the framing.

Note: There are some important options to consider when you apply a Layer Style that includes a pattern or texture effect:

• First, certain Scale percentages work best for keeping the surface markings or texture of a Layer Style sharp and clear. (Each **One-Click Wow! Style** that includes a pattern or texture has an **asterisk [*]** after its name in the examples shown on pages 48–51 and 60–83 of this book.) If you've made sure that the Resolution setting of your file is 225 pixels/inch (as described in the tip on page 17), these optimal percentages are 25%, 50%, 100% (no scaling), and 200%. If none of these percentages

▶ *It's possible to scale a Layer Style so small that some of its features go away—for instance, the bevel or drop shadow could disappear if you were to set a very low Scale value in the Scale Effects dialog box and then click OK to close the box. Once you've scaled a file too small, you may not be able to successfully scale it up again. If that happens, you can simply apply the Style again and scale again, this time not as small.*

is ideal for your project, you may need to accept a somewhat soft-looking pattern in order to get the ideal width of the frame, for instance. (Styles that *don't* include a surface pattern or texture don't have an asterisk in their names, and you don't have to worry about restricting the Scale setting to one of these values.)

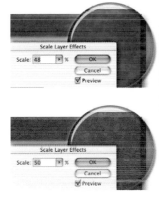

Scaling the **Wow-Frame 03** Style to 48% blurs the pattern (top), but using a Scale factor of exactly 50% keeps the pattern sharp.

• Second, when you reduce the Scale of a patterned or textured Style, **the repeat in the pattern may become more apparent.** For instance, if you look carefully at the frame around Great Grandma's portrait in step 2 on page 16, you can see that the repeating pattern that's used to create the texture is more obvious than it was in step 1, when the Style was first applied at the default 100% Scale setting.

If you apply a **One-Click Wow! Style** to a file whose Resolution is *not* set to 225 pixels/inch, you may get a result that looks different from the corresponding sample shown in this book. Here are some examples of **Wow-Frame 03** applied to exactly the same file but with four different, commonly used Resolution settings:

72 pixels/inch

150 pixels/inch

225 pixels/inch

300 pixels/inch

Note that changing a file's Resolution in order to scale a Style isn't an efficient approach. Instead, it's much more effective to use the scaling method described in step 2 starting on page 16. But if you apply a **One-Click Wow! Style** to a file whose Resolution is *not* set at 225 pixels/inch, here are some settings you can use in the Scale Layer Effects dialog box in order to help keep it sharp if it has a pattern. The percentages in bold type will produce the same results as the default 100% Scale in a 225 pixels/inch file. (Again, for Styles without a surface pattern or texture, you don't have to worry about using these special Scale settings.)

72 pixels/inch: 78%, 156%, **312%**, 624%
150 pixels/inch: 75%, **150%**, 300%
300 pixels/inch: **75%**, 150%, 300%

Customizing Styles

Photoshop lets you change the component effects of a Style you've applied, or even add more effects. Then you can save your customized Style for future use.

▶ *The aim of this book is to show what can be done with the Presets on the **One-Click Wow! CD-ROM**, and to explain how to use them. For complete coverage of Layer Styles, including how to create them from scratch and how to work with the Blending Options, we recommend the most recent edition of* **The Photoshop Wow! Book***, especially the chapter on "Special Effects for Type & Graphics."*

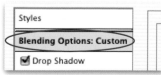

In addition to the effects, a Layer Style includes Blending Options that control how the Style and the layer interact with other layers and with masks.

If you don't find *exactly* the Layer Style you want among the **One-Click Wow! Styles**, you can apply one that's close to what you want and then modify it. The Layer Style dialog box is where you make changes to a Style after you've applied it to a layer.

You can open the Layer Style dialog box (below) by double-clicking the ● to the right of the "styled" layer's name in the Layers palette or by double-clicking any of the effects in the expanded list underneath.

On the left side of the Layer Style dialog box are all the effects that can be included in a Style. Those that are actually included in the current Style have check marks in the boxes next to their names. Add or remove an effect by clicking its check box. Clicking the name of the effect turns on the effect and opens the appropriate section of the Layer Style box so you can customize it.

To customize an effect, it helps to know what that effect does. Here's a brief intro:

• The **Shadows** and **Glows** add soft darkening or lightening effects around the edges of whatever the layer contains. You can change whether they are dark or light by changing their color and Blend Mode. You can also adjust their softness or density. Two characteristics can't be changed:

(1) The **Drop Shadow** and **Outer Glow** extend **outward** from the edge, but the **Inner Shadow** and **Inner Glow** extend **inward**; and (2) the **Glows always extend evenly** in all directions, whereas the **Shadows can be offset**.

*The **Wow-Frame 07** Style includes a typical dark Drop Shadow.*

*In **Wow-Glow 02** a bright purple Drop Shadow in Screen mode adds to the neon glow.*

• The settings in the **Bevel And Emboss** section of the Layer Style box interact to create beveled edges, and the settings in the **Contour** and **Texture** "subeffects" can also contribute. The **Contour** is important in shaping the "shoulder" of the bevel, and the **Texture** can add surface "bump."

*In **Wow-Metal 15** the Contour helps shape the edge, and the Texture makes the surface bumpy.*

• The **Satin** effect can add complex "interior" lighting in a translucent Style or reflections in an opaque Style.

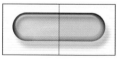

Wow-Plastic 09 with its built-in Satin effect turned on (left) to create refracted light and turned off (right)

In Wow-Chrome 20 the built-in Satin effect simulates reflections (left); turning Satin off dulls the chrome.

• **Overlay** effects apply **Color**, **Gradient**, and **Pattern**, which are "stacked" in that top-to-bottom order if more than one is applied.

▶ With the Layer Style dialog box open to a particular effect's section, there are some things you can change without using the sliders or typing numbers—just by dragging the cursor in your image. For instance, you can drag to change the Angle and offset Distance of a Drop Shadow or an Inner Shadow, or to reposition the Texture subeffect, the Satin effect, the Gradient Overlay or Pattern Overlay, or the coloring for most kinds of Gradient- or Pattern-based Strokes.

▶ Besides changing the individual component effects in a Style, you can also scale all the effects in the Style together, or resize an entire "styled" file, keeping all the Styles in proportion, as described in *"Scaling a Style"* on pages 16–17.

▶ Clicking the Styles button at the top of the list in the Layer Style dialog box opens the current Styles palette—right inside the box!

In **Wow-Woods 15** the Pattern Overlay creates the woodgrain (left), the Gradient Overlay in Color Dodge mode adds lighting (center), and a dark yellow Color Overlay in Overlay mode subtly enhances color and contrast.

- The **Stroke** effect outlines the edges with Color, a Gradient, or even a Pattern. The stroke can be inside, outside, or straddling the edge.

The neon tubing of **Wow-Glow 01** is created with a Shape Burst gradient Stroke.

Once you've applied a Style, you can make changes in the Layer Style box to modify it. Here are just a few examples:

- You can make an element look farther "above" the surface simply by increasing the Distance of the Drop Shadow.

In the **Wow-Fabric 16** Style, increasing the Drop Shadow effect's Distance setting from the built-in 9 px (pixels) (left) to 36 px makes the type seem to float higher above the page.

- You can change the lighting direction by changing the Angle setting for the Drop Shadow, Inner Shadow, and Bevel And Emboss. (If you change one of these, you'll need to change all of them in order to keep the Style's lighting consistent.)

Changing the Angle for the Drop Shadow effect in **Wow-Chrome 13** from the built-in 120 degrees (left) to –60 degrees (right) changes the light source from upper left to lower right.

- You can change the molding of a picture frame Style by choosing a different Contour in the Contour subeffect's section.

Changing from the relatively simple built-in Contour used for the Contour subeffect of Bevel And Emboss (left) to a more complex Contour (right) changes the molding of the frame created by **Wow-Frame 04**.

- In a Style that uses the same Pattern choice for the Pattern Overlay and the Texture subeffect, you can smooth the surface by turning off the Texture.

The **Wow-Plastic 03** Style with its built-in Texture subeffect (left) and without it (right)

After you've made changes to a Style, you can save it for future use. First add it to the current Styles palette. Then use the Preset Manager to save it as part of a Styles library.

👁 See step 8 of "A Layer Style Tutorial" on page 31 to learn how to name and save Styles.

Copying & Pasting Styles

Copy Styles from layer to layer or file to file.

▶ *When you copy a Style from one file and paste it to another, you're much more likely to get the same "look" if the two files have the same Resolution setting. (Remember, all the **One-Click Wow! Styles** except the **Wow-Button Styles** were created at a standard 225 pixels/inch.) A quick way to find a file's Resolution is to Alt/Option-click the description entry in the lower left corner of the working window.*

*If the Resolution settings of your files are different and you need to temporarily change the Resolution setting of the "recipient" file to match that of the "donor," choose Image > Image Size, **make sure "Resample Image" is turned OFF**, and type in the Resolution setting from the donor file. (Follow the same procedure to reset the Resolution back to its original value after you paste the Style.)*

It's easy to copy a Style from one layer and apply it to other layers, in the same file or a different one. This makes it possible to reproduce a Style that you create "from scratch" or one that you find already applied in a file. Here's how you can go about copying and pasting a Style:

1 To copy a Style, right-click (Windows) or Ctrl-click (Mac) on the *ƒ* icon to the right of the layer's name to open a context-sensitive menu where you can choose Copy Layer Style. (Another option is to **choose Layer > Layer Style > Copy Layer Style.**)

*We liked the Style that we found on the "Dinner" layer of this photo collage (it's a scaled version of **Wow-Edges 05**), and we wanted to apply it to other layers.*

We used the context-sensitive menu to copy the Style.

2 To paste the copied Style, right-click (Windows) or Ctrl-click (Mac) to the right of the name of a layer where you want to apply the Style. The context-sensitive menu will re-open, and you can **choose Paste Layer Style.**

We pasted the copied Style to another layer, again using the context-sensitive menu.

3 Continue pasting to any other layers where you want to apply the Style. If you want to copy and paste a Style to more than two layers, in Photoshop CS2, you can save time by first Ctrl/⌘ clicking on the desired layers to select them (or in earlier versions of Photoshop you can "link" these target layers together by clicking in the column just to the left of the thumbnail) and then use the context-sensitive menu again to **Paste Layer Style** (in CS or earlier choose Paste Layer Style To Linked).

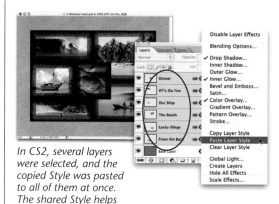

In CS2, several layers were selected, and the copied Style was pasted to all of them at once. The shared Style helps unify the six assembled images.

Using Styles with Layer & Clipping Masks

Layer masks, vector masks, and clipping masks provide a way to mask an image inside any shape or type.

▶ **In Photoshop there are several ways to add a vector mask to a layer. First target the layer in the Layers palette.**

• **Then you can use the main menu—choose Layer > Add Vector Mask.**

• **Or you can Ctrl/⌘-click the "Add a mask" button at the bottom of the palette.**

• **If you've already added a layer mask to the layer, Photoshop is smart enough to know that a vector mask is the only masking option that's left. So you can leave out the Ctrl/⌘ and click the "Add a mask" button.**

In Photoshop, each layer (except *Background*) can have two masks—a pixel-based *layer mask* and an outline-based *vector mask*. These masks determine which parts of the layer will show and which will be hidden.

You can add a vector mask to a layer by Ctrl/⌘-clicking the "Add a mask" button at the bottom of the Layers palette. Then choose a Shape tool (such as the Ellipse) from the Tools palette, click the "Add to path area (+)" button ▣▣▣▣ in the Options bar, and drag to draw the mask.

By default, a layer mask or vector mask is linked to the layer content. So, for example, if you drag the image with the Move tool, its mask will move also, and the same area of the image will remain showing. But if you break the link by clicking the link icon between the image thumbnail and mask thumbnail, then when you move the image, the mask will stay stationary, and a different part of the image will be revealed.

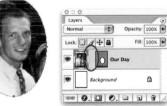

When the link is broken between an image and its mask as shown here, you can reposition the image inside the mask by dragging with the Move tool in the working window.

When a "styled" layer has either kind of mask, by default any edge effects in the Style will follow the edges of the mask.

The **Wow-Tint FX 03** *Style creates a partial sepiatone and adds an interior glow and a drop shadow around the edges. Our vector mask serves as the edge to which the glow is applied.*

If you modify the mask, as shown below, the Style conforms to the new shape.

The ellipse was reshaped to contain both people by choosing the Path Selection tool (the solid arrow just above the Pen in the Tools palette), pressing Ctrl/⌘-T, and dragging a corner of the box.

You can turn *off* a mask's influence on *edge effects* by turning *on* "Layer Mask Hides Effects" or "Vector Mask Hides Effects" in the Blending Options section of the Layer Styles dialog box.

 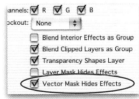

Turning on "Vector Mask Hides Effects" in the Blending Options section of the Layer Style dialog box hides the glow and shadow.

Using Styles with Layer & Clipping Masks

continued

▶ *When you want to make a clipping mask from layers that are stacked up in your Photoshop file, there are several ways to go about it:*

- *In the Layers palette you can target the layer above your soon-to-be "clipping" layer, then from Photoshop's main menu choose Layer > Create Clipping Mask.*

- *Or target the layer and use the keyboard shortcut for Create Clipping Mask, which is Ctrl/Alt-G or ⌘/Option-G.*

- *You can hold down the Alt/Option key and move the cursor over the border between the "clipping" layer and the layer above it. When the cursor changes to the double-circle clipping icon, click to form the clipping mask.*

You can add more layers to a clipping mask simply by working sequentially up the stack of layers in the Layers palette, using any of the methods above.

A *clipping mask* (called a *clipping group* in earlier versions of Photoshop) allows you to use the content of one layer as a mask for a different layer (or layers) above it. 👁 *See the tip at the left for three methods for forming a clipping mask.* When you create a clipping mask, in the Layers palette the name of the "cookie cutter" (clipping) layer is underlined, and the name of the clipped layer is indented.

U sing a clipping mask can have certain advantages over using a layer mask or vector mask. One is that with a clipping group you can mask an image inside type and still keep the type "live" and changeable.

You can make a clipping mask by Alt/Option-clicking between layers as shown here. Any Style applied to the "clipping" layer will also apply to the "clipped" layer above it. In this case the **Wow-Glass 12** *Style was applied to the "Seaside" type layer.*

By default, in a clipping mask if you move (or scale or rotate) the "clipped" layer, the "clipping" layer below doesn't move with it.

The image was rotated inside the type by clicking on the photo layer in the Layers palette, then pressing Ctrl/⌘-T (for Edit > Free Transform) and dragging clockwise on a corner handle of the Transform box.

This makes it easy to reposition the clipped image inside the clipping type or shape.

However, if you want to move (or scale or rotate) both layers, you can do so by either simply selecting the multiple layers in the Layers palette and doing the transformation, or linking the selected layers (so they stay connected even when not actively selected), then move, rotate, or scale any one of them to affect them all together.

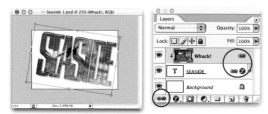 

The photo layer was targeted and the "Seaside" type layer was linked to it. Then the Free Transform command was used to rotate both layers together.

A nother advantage of making a clipping mask is that you can use it to mask (and "style") more than one layer.

 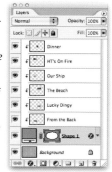

Each of the six photos in this collage (above left) is on a separate layer. All of the layers were added to a clipping mask with an Ellipse Shape layer as its base (clipping) layer, and the **Wow-Tint FX 08** *Style was applied to this layer. The Style affects all of the "clipped" photos, adding a slight tint and a "pebbled" surface texture and darkening their clipped edges.*

Working with Styles in Image-Ready

Use Styles in ImageReady to add dimension and interactivity to button graphics.

▶ *In ImageReady, by default the list of individual effects in a Style is **not** displayed in the Layers palette. Click the little triangle to the left of the ✪ icon to show the list.*

▶ *Rollover Styles are designed to be used In ImageReady. If you apply a Rollover Style in Photoshop, only the Normal state will be applied and it will not be interactive.*

▶ *It's a good idea to keep button labels on a separate layer from the button graph-ics. That way you can keep the type "live" and even give the type layer a separate "single" Style of its own.*

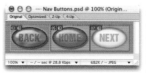

In ImageReady you load and apply Styles just as you do in Photoshop. But in addi-tion to the "single" Styles you can apply in Photoshop, in ImageReady you can also apply and customize *Rollover Styles.*

In the **Wow-20 Button Styles** library (designed especially for use in ImageReady), the Styles whose names include the words "**All Three**" are Rollover Styles.

To apply a Style in ImageReady, choose a Styles library from the Styles palette's pop-out menu, target a layer in the Layers palette, and then click the Style you want in the Styles palette. (Rollover Styles have a small black mark in the upper-left corner of the thumbnail.)

When you apply one of the **Wow Button-All Three** Styles to a layer, an interactive rectangular *slice* is created, big enough to in clude everything in the styled layer that isn't transparent. The slice automatically responds to what the user does with the cursor. Each **Wow Button-All Three** Style has **Normal**, **Over**, and **Down** states. ☜ *See "What Is a Layer Style?" on page 13 for definitions of these three states.*

*Applying **Wow Button-All Three** Styles to three buttons, each in its own layer, created a layer-based slice for each graphic.*

ImageReady CS2's Web Content palette makes it easy to target a particular state in a Rollover Style you've applied, so you can examine it or make changes. For instance:

- To view (and target) a particular state, click on its name in the Slices portion of the Web Content palette.

In the Web Content palette, click the little triangle to the left of the Normal State's entry to show the other states in the Rollover. Click on a particular state's thumbnail to target that state.

- To replace the Style used for the targeted state, you can click a single (non-Rollover) Style in the Styles palette.

- To edit one or more effects of the targeted state's Style, target the appropriate layer in the Layers palette, then double-click the name of the effect in the Layers palette to open that effect's palette. (Single-state Styles can also be customized this way.)

Double-clicking on a Layer Style icon brings up the Layer Style dia-log where a plethora of customizing possibilities awaits you.

- To keep the Style but change the state it represents, double-click the name of the state and choose from the Rollover State Options dialog box.

Choosing a different state

Saving, Sizing & Output

For maximum flexibility, save your layered and "styled" file in Photoshop format. Then choose the right size and file format for output for:

- *printing directly from Photoshop*
- *placing your image in another program for printing*
- *doing further work to the file in ImageReady*
- *displaying the image on-screen*

As you work on "styling" a file in Photoshop, it's a good idea to save the file periodically in the native Photoshop (.psd) format. This will keep "alive" and "editable" all the information that you build into the file—including type, layers and Layer Styles—so you can go back and make changes to them later if you like.

Save your layered file. The first time you save your file, **choose File > Save As.** In the Save As dialog box, **choose Photoshop** for the Format; make sure the **"As a Copy" box is NOT checked** and the **"Layers" box IS checked**, so the layers and Layer Styles will be preserved. Name the file, choose where you want to store it, and then click the **Save** button.

Photoshop's Save As dialog box (Mac OS X), set up for saving a layered file in the flexible Photoshop format

For subsequent saves as you work on the file, simply **choose File > Save** or **press Ctrl/⌘-S.** The file will be resaved in Photoshop format.

When you've finished applying and customizing Layer Styles and you've saved your finished file in Photoshop format, it's easy to get it sized for printing, then print directly from Photoshop, or ready to place in a page layout or word-processing program. (If you want to further work on your file in ImageReady, go to "Reducing a copy of the layered file for further work in ImageReady" on page 26. Or if you simply want to send your file as an email attachment or post it on a Web page, go to "Resizing for email or for the Web" on page 27.)

Whether you'll be printing directly from Photoshop or placing a file in another program and printing from there, you can use the Image Size dialog box to figure out whether you can get good results by printing the image "as is" or whether you'll need to change its dimensions before you print.

Check the size of your file for printing. To open the Image Size dialog box, choose **Image > Image Size.** Make sure the "Resample Image" box is *not* checked. 👁 *The tip on page 25 tells why turning off "Resample Image" is important.*

If the size you want is different from the current Width and Height settings shown in the Document Size section of the box, **type in the Width or Height** value you want. The other dimension will change automatically to keep the image in proportion, and the **Resolution** setting will change also.

If the new Resolution setting is *at least* as high as one of the following, your file has plenty of information for printing at the size you've entered. As a rule of thumb:
- A safe Resolution setting for inkjet printing is **150 pixels/inch** or higher.
- A safe Resolution setting for commercial printing on a press is **225 pixels/inch** or higher.

▶ *With "Resample Image" turned OFF in the Image Size dialog box, **none of the changes you make in the dialog box will change the color of any of the pixels** (the square dots that make up the image file). For example, if you **reduce the Width and Height dimensions,** the Resolution setting will increase. Basically, you are telling Photoshop to keep each of the pixels exactly the same color it is, but print all the pixels smaller. That way each one will take up less space and they can be packed more tightly to make a smaller, sharper printed image.*

*On the other hand, if you **increase the dimensions,** again the pixels aren't changed, but they will be printed larger. You just need to be careful that pixel size doesn't get so large—in other words Resolution (pixels/inch) doesn't get so low—that the pixels themselves can be seen, usually as jagged edges in areas of contrast.*

A file that doesn't have enough pixels/inch is likely to show pixel artifacts. This is especially likely when the image is printed on a press.

If your file's Resolution setting falls in one of these "safe" zones, you can proceed to "Printing directly from Photoshop" or "Preparing a duplicate file to place in another program" (both at the right).

Resizing the file for printing if you need to.
If your file's Resolution setting is less than the appropriate "safe" value on page 24, it may not make a crisp and clean print.

The low Resolution value in the Image Size dialog box means that if this file were to be printed at 8 x 10 inches, the print might look "pixelated" (with visibly jagged edges).

An easy way to improve print quality is to raise the Resolution setting into the safe range by setting up the file to print smaller: Reduce the Width/Height dimensions until the Resolution rises to a safe number.

Reducing the Width and Height to 5 x 4 inches raised the Resolution setting high enough so this file could be printed on an inkjet printer.

By reducing the dimensions with "Resample Image" turned OFF, you are telling Photoshop to keep each pixel (tiny square dot) in

the image exactly the same color but make all the pixels print smaller so they can be packed tighter (more pixels/inch) on the printed page and the viewer's eye won't be able to detect the individual square dots in the printed image.

Printing directly from Photoshop.
Once your dimensions are set and your Resolution setting is safe, if you're printing directly from Photoshop, you're all set. All you have to do is **choose File > Print With Preview**, check the position of the image on the page, and **click Print** (or click Page Setup if you need to rotate the page orientation). Then make sure that your printer's options are set up to best match the paper you're using. Some printers also have advanced options for improving the print quality of photos or artwork.

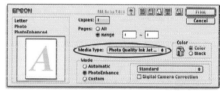

The Epson C80's driver software can tell whether your image is color or black-and-white, but you have to tell it what kind of paper you're using (here photo-quality inkjet paper). This printer's PhotoEnhance mode works well for photos and many other images.

Preparing a duplicate file to place in another program.
If your image will be placed in a page layout program and printed from there, you'll need to do just a little more work. One good way to prepare a file for printing from another program is to save a flattened copy (a *flattened* file is one that consists only of a single *Background* layer).

First, to make a duplicate copy to flatten, **choose Image > Duplicate.**

Duplicating the file

Saving, Sizing
& Output
continued

▶ *As a rule of thumb, here are some of the most useful file formats for saving projects in Photoshop:*

• *To keep all layers and Styles "alive" or to print an image from within Photoshop, save in **Photoshop** (or .psd) format.*

• *If your goal is to place the image on a page in a page layout program, **TIFF** (.tif) works well in most cases.*

• *Because it can reduce file size so effectively, **JPEG** (.jpg) is a good format for posting on the Web or for attaching to an email. Note that JPEG compression can cause a noticeable reduction in image quality.*

• *If you want your file to be readable with Adobe Acrobat Reader (a widely used free application that works on both Windows and Mac), save in **Photoshop PDF** (.pdf) format.*

*To read more about formats for saving files, in Photoshop **choose Help > Photoshop Help** and **choose the "Saving and Exporting Images"** topic from the Contents.*

Then, to flatten this copy, **choose Layer > Flatten Image**. This will make a single-*Background*-layer version of your file. The image will look the same as the layered file, but the separate layers and Styles will no longer be available for changing. Transparency will be replaced with white, and type will no longer be "live." (That's why it was important to flatten a *copy* but also to save the original "live" file in Photoshop format as described in "Saving your layered file" on page 24.)

To save this duplicate file, **choose File > Save As** and select an appropriate format, such as **TIFF**, from the Format list in the Save As dialog box 👁 *See the tip at the left for help on choosing a file format.* Name the file, choose where you want to save it, and **click Save.**

❙ f your duplicate file will ultimately be displayed on the screen (instead of being printed)—as part of an animation or interactive interface, as an attachment to email, or an image for a Web page, for instance—consider reducing its pixel dimensions so the entire image will fit, even on a small screen.

Reduce a copy of the layered file for further work in ImageReady. Perhaps you'd like to bring a fully layered and "styled" version of your file into ImageReady so you can make buttons, or so you can turn various layers on and off in building an animation. If so, you should preserve the Layer Styles by reducing the size of the file in Photoshop first: Make a duplicate of the layered file in Photoshop by **choosing Image > Duplicate and clicking OK.**

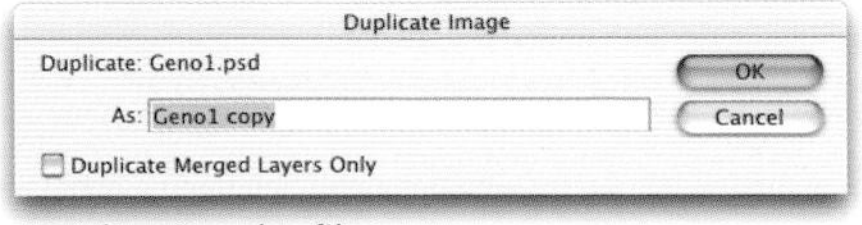

Duplicating the file

What you must do next will seem a bit convoluted, but it's important to do it as described because of the strange and wonderful relationship between Photoshop's Layer Styles and the Resolution setting. The secret is to **change the Resolution (pixels/inch setting),** *not* **the pixel dimensions:**

1 **Figure out a target pixel dimension** for either Width or Height. For instance, you may need to make the file exactly 464 pixels high for a particular project.

2 **Working in the duplicate file,** open the Image Size dialog box (**Image > Image Size**). **Turn "Resample Image" ON and** also **turn "Constrain Proportions" ON.**

3 In the image Size dialog box **change the Resolution setting—not the Height or Width setting**—until the critical number (Height or Width) at the top of the box matches the target you figured out in step 1. You can use decimal fractions for the Resolution to arrive at exactly the right number of pixels for Height or Width.

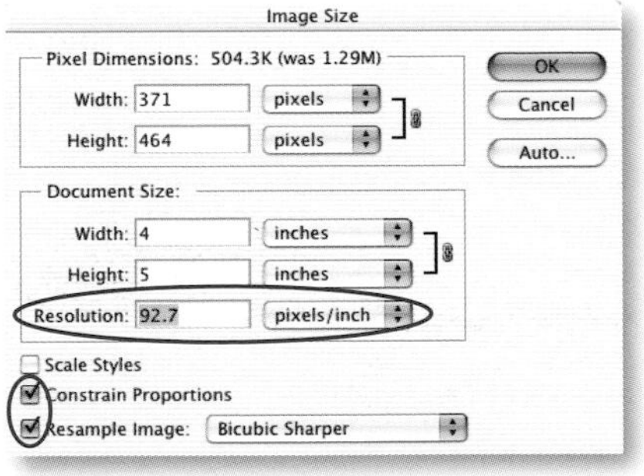

Watch the "pixels" settings at the top of the dialog box as you use a trial-and-error method to arrive at a Resolution setting that will produce your target number of pixels for Width or Height (here 464 pixels).

4 Click OK to complete the resizing and close the dialog box. The image will have been resized, and any Styles in the file will have been scaled along with it.

▶ *With "Resample Image" turned ON in the Image Size dialog box, **changing the Height and Width dimensions actually changes the number of pixels in the file:** Photoshop "throws away" some pixels to make the image smaller. To make it so this scaling doesn't soften your file, make sure that you have your Photoshop Preferences set to Bicubic Sharper under the Image Interpolation option.*

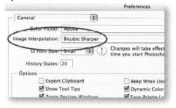

To move the resized file to ImageReady, **click the "Jump to ImageReady" button** at the very bottom of Photoshop's Tools palette.

Resize for email or for the Web. The difference between preparing a layered file for further work in ImageReady and preparing a file to be attached to email or posted on the Web is that you start by making a flattened, rather than layered, duplicate of your "styled" Photoshop file: **Choose Image > Duplicate, click OK,** and then **choose Layer > Flatten Image.** 👁 *See "Preparing a duplicate file to place in another program" on page 25–26 for more about flattening a file.*

Working in the new flattened copy of the file, Open the Image Size dialog box (**choose Image > Image Size**). **Turn** "Resample Image" ON and also **turn** "Constrain Proportions" ON. In the **Pixel Dimensions** section at the top of the box, type in the appropriate number of pixels for **Width** or **Height**. If you haven't been told what pixel dimensions to use, limiting the Width to no more than 580 pixels and the Height to no more than 400 pixels will create a file that will display the entire image, even on a small screen.

The "Resample Image" option must be turned ON in order to make it possible to change the Pixel Dimensions.

Sharpen and Save. Changing the dimensions of a file with "Resample Image" turned ON can cause the image to look slightly fuzzy—UNLESS you make sure that you have your Photoshop Preferences set to Bicubic Sharper under the Image Interpolation option.

Instead of using File > Save As, you can optimize the image (reduce the file size as small as possible without losing too much image quality) by using **File > Save For Web.** (To learn about using Save For Web, **choose Help > How to Create Web Images > To optimize an image for the web.**

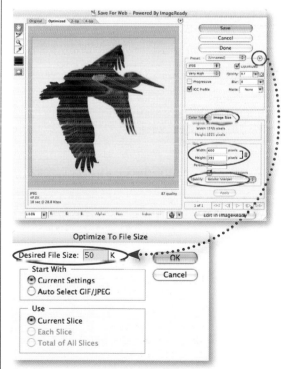

Two of the great features of the current Save for Web are its ability to scale an image to a specific Image Size (even using Bicubic Sharper!) and to a specific File Size.

A Layer Style Tutorial

Learn how to:

1 Set up Photoshop to work with Styles

2 Apply Styles

3 Alter a Style

4 Copy and paste a Style

5 Convert a Background so you can apply a Style

6 Replace a Style

7 Scale a Style

8 Save a library of Style presets

9 Change layer content but keep the Style

10 Add a Rollover Style in Image-Ready

1 Prepare the file. Make sure the **One-Click Wow! Styles** are installed. 👁 *See "One-Click Wow! Quick Start" on page 3 for directions for installing Styles.*

Start Photoshop and make sure the Layers palette is open (if not, **choose Window > Layers**). Open the Styles palette in the same way (**choose Window > Styles**). Click the little triangle in the top-right corner of the Styles palette and choose Large List.

For each Style, the Styles palette's Large List view shows a thumbnail plus the Style's full name. The bottom section of the pop-out menu lists all the Styles libraries in Photoshop's Styles folder.

Now use the Styles palette's pop-out menu again to **load Wow-15 Organic Styles** from the libraries at the bottom of the menu; in the caution box that appears, **click the Append button** to *add* this library to your currently loaded Styles, **or click OK** to *replace* them. 👁 *See the tip on page 29 about appending versus replacing.* Then **append the Wow-03 Tint FX Styles and the Wow-17 Stroke Styles.**

Click Append to add to the current Styles in the Styles palette; click OK to replace them.

Next, copy the **Wow-Styles Tutorial 1.psd** file from the **Wow-Styles Tutorial** folder on the **One-Click Wow! CD-ROM** onto your hard disk drive. Then open this file (**choose File > Open**).

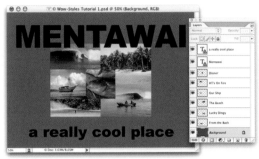

*The **Wow-Styles Tutorial 1.psd** file*

With the Layers palette open, you can see that the **Wow-Styles Tutorial 1.psd file**, which is a postcard layout, has each of its components on a separate layer:

- Type, in the Arial Black font, has been set in two separate layers so different Styles can be applied to the two settings.

- The photos are all on separate layers also, but they have all been *linked*, by clicking on one layer's name in the Layers palette and then clicking in the "links" column to the left of the thumbnail for each of the other photos. This allows all the photos to be moved or "styled" together.

- At the bottom of the stack of layers is a gray-filled *Background*.

None of the layers in this file has a Style applied to it yet.

2 Apply Layer Styles. With each element on a layer of its own, you'll be able to add color and dimension by applying different Styles to the individual layers:

- For the "Mentawai" type layer, in the Styles palette click **Wow-Organics 05**, a

▶ *When you apply a Style to a layer, the ⚫ icon appears to the right of the name in the Layers palette. Also, indented under the layer's name is a list of the individual effects that make up the Style. You can click on the "eye" icon next to any effect to temporarily turn off the effect. Click in this column again to toggle the effect back on. To make the Layers palette more compact, you can also click the tiny triangle to the left of the ⚫ to hide the list of effects; clicking again expands the list.*

▶ *When you open a library of Styles, you have the choice of appending (adding) the new Styles to the ones that are already in the Styles palette, or replacing the current Styles with the new ones. Each choice has advantages and disadvantages. Appending can lead to a very long list that can tie up RAM and also make it hard to find a particular Style. On the other hand, if you replace the current set of Styles rather than adding on, you risk losing any Styles that you've created, imported, or modified and added to the list but haven't yet saved as part of a library.*

dimensional Style that includes shadows, glows, a photographic Pattern Overlay (the weave), and a tint created by a Color Overlay.

• For "a really cool place" use **Wow-Stroke 01**, made with three Overlays: Color, Gradient, and Pattern.

• For the central ("Dinner") photo layer, use **Wow-Tint FX 01**, a "partial sepiatone" Style made with a white inner glow, a dark drop shadow, and a color overlay that partially replaces color with brown tones.

*The **Wow-Styles Tutorial 1.psd** file after Styles have been applied to the two type layers and the "Dinner" photo layer. In the Layers palette, small ⚫ icons mark the "styled" layers.*

3 Customize a Style. It's easy to modify a Style once you've applied it. To change the Style for the "Dinner" photo layer, **double-click the ⚫ icon** next to its name in the Layers palette to open the Layer Styles dialog

*The built-in Size setting for the Inner Glow in the **Wow-Tint FX 01** Style is 32 px (pixels).*

box. Then **click "Inner Glow"** in the list on the left side of the box to see the settings.

Reduce the Inner Glow's Size setting to 10 px (pixels) to shrink the edge effect. **Click OK** to close the dialog box.

Before (left) and after reducing the Inner Glow's Size setting to 10 px

4 Copy and paste a Style. To apply this modified Style to the other photo layers, **copy and paste it, as follows: Right-click (Windows) or Ctrl-click (Mac) the ⚫ icon for the "Dinner" layer,** and when the context-sensitive menu appears, **choose Copy Layer Style.** Then, since the other photos are already linked, simply **right/Ctrl-click the ⚫ icon for any other photo layer** and **choose Paste Layer Style To Linked,** and all the photos will share the same Style. (For pasting a Style to a *single layer,* the choice would be Paste Layer Style.)

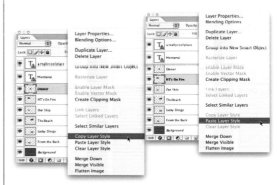

Copying the Style (left) and pasting it to the other linked photo layers (right)

A Layer Style Tutorial
continued

▶ *In Photoshop, double-clicking the **name** of the layer selects the name itself so you can edit it to rename the layer.*

*But double-clicking **the image thumbnail** or **the ❶ icon** will open the Layer Style dialog box so you can customize a Style that has been applied to the layer.*

*And, like any Layer Style, all these 150 **Wow-Button** Styles work great on any graphic or text—not just buttons!*

*Below, the **Wow Button 02-Normal** Style was applied to the "A," the **Wow Button 40-Over** was used on the "B," and **Wow Button 05-Down** was used on the "C." All the Styles were scaled to fit the type.*

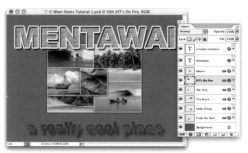

*The **Wow-Styles Tutorial 1.psd** file after the **Wow-Tint FX 01** Style has been pasted to the linked layers*

5 Convert a *Background*.
To make an "instant background," you can use a One-Click Wow! Style to fill an entire layer with a pattern consisting of an image or texture. But to replace the gray background of the Wow-Styles Tutorial 1.psd file you're working on, you first have to turn the *Background* into a layer that can accept a Style. To do this, **double-click the *Background's* thumbnail in the Layers palette**, type a new layer name in the New Layer dialog box if you like (such as "Base Layer"), and **click OK**.

Converting the Background

To turn the "Base Layer" into bamboo, click **Wow-Organics 16** in the Styles palette.

*The file after the **Wow-Organics 16** Style has been applied to the bottom layer (The **Wow-Styles Tutorial 2.psd** file shows the project at this stage.)*

6 Replace Styles.
One of the great advantages of Layer Styles is that you can change the entire "look and feel" of a Photoshop composition instantly, simply by replacing some of the Layer Styles. To target the layer whose Style you want to change, click its name in the Layers palette. Then load the appropriate **One-Click Wow! Styles** library into the Styles palette (as in step 1) and click on a new Style. For instance:

- To change the Style for the "Base Layer," load **Wow-14 Rock Styles** and choose **Wow-Rocks 20**, a complex sandstone-like texture.
- For the "Mentawai" type, **load Wow-09 Metal Styles** and **apply Wow-Metals 06**, a golden metallic treatment that includes a Pattern Overlay and a matching Texture.

*On the "Mentawai" type and the "Base Layer," new Styles (**Wow-Metals 06** and **Wow-Rock 20**, respectively) have replaced the old ones.*

7 Scaling a Style.
Scaling often helps to "custom-fit" a Style to a specific graphic. In the Layers palette, **click "a really cool place"** to target this layer. Then **right-click** (Windows) or **Ctrl-click** (Mac) the ❶ icon to the right of the layer's name and **choose Scale Effects** from the context-sensitive menu. In the Scale Layer Effects dialog box, **click the little triangle** to the right of the "100" to pop out the slider. Then **move the slider to the left** to scale the pattern and

► *If you want to create a library of Styles that includes some or all of the ones currently in the Styles palette,* **choose Edit > Preset Manager** *and* **choose Styles** *from the pop-out Preset Type menu to display the current Styles. Then Shift-click the Styles that you want to include, and click the "Save Set" button.*

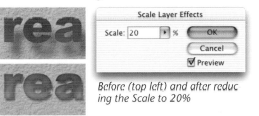

Clicking "Save Set" to create a library from the selected Styles

When the Save dialog box appears, name your new library, navigate to the Styles folder (Inside Photoshop's Presets folder) and click the Save button.

Saving the new library into the Styles folder so it will automatically appear in the Styles palette's pop-out menu

reduce the offset of the drop shadow. Moving the shadow makes the lettering seem closer to the background.

Scale Layer Effects
Scale: 20 % OK / Cancel / ☑ Preview

Before (top left) and after reducing the Scale to 20%

8 Save a library of Styles. When you alter a Style you've applied, such as the modified partial sepiatone made in step 3 or the scaled Style in step 7), it's a good idea to give the new Style its own name and save it as part of a Styles library. That way, you can choose it directly from the Styles palette in the future. Saving a custom Style is a two-step process:

• First, add the Style to the list of Styles currently displayed in the Styles palette: **Target the layer that has the Style** you want to save (such as the "Dinner" layer), then **click the "Create new style" button** at the bottom of the Styles palette. In the New Style dialog box, leave the check boxes set as they are, **name the Style,** and **click OK.**

Styles
🔲 Wow–Metals 06*
🔲 Wow–Metals 07*

New Style
Name: Wow-Sepia Alternative 1   OK
☑ Include Layer Effects   Cancel
☐ Include Layer Blending Options

With the "styled" layer targeted, clicking the "Create new style" button starts the process of saving the current Style. When you close the New Style box, your Style will appear in the last position in the Styles palette.

• To protect your new Style from being lost if you replace the current Styles, **choose Edit > Preset Manager** and **choose Styles** from the Preset Type menu in the Preset Manager dialog box. Now you can create a new library that includes any or all of the currently loaded Styles.  *See the tip at the left for directions on saving a new library of Styles.* When you've finished saving libraries, **click the Done button.**

9 Change layer content. Part of the magic of Layer Styles is that they "stick with" the layer. So if you change the content of a layer to which a Style has been applied, the Style instantly conforms to the new content:

• To change the font in the "Mentawai" layer, **target this layer** in the Layers palette, then **choose the Type tool and choose a new font** from the pop-up list in the Options bar. (If you want to change the font for the entire layer, as we do here, there's no need to select any text with the cursor.)

T ▾ | ⊥T | CCDutchCourage ▾ | Dark ▾

Before (top) and after changing the font (If you don't have the CCDutchCourage font, use another font of your choice.)

• To change the wording in the "a really cool place" layer, **target this layer, drag the Type tool cursor over the type** to select it, **press the Caps Lock key,** and **type** "BEYOND THE DREAM"; **press the Enter key** to finalize the change.

A Layer Style Tutorial
continued

▶ *The Styles palettes in Photoshop and ImageReady are similar, but not exactly the same. For instance:*

- *Loading a library of Styles in one program doesn't automatically load it in the other program. You have to load the two programs' Styles palettes separately.*

- *Unlike Photoshop, ImageReady doesn't have a Large List option for the styles palette display. So the Small List option is best for seeing both a "swatch" of each Style and the Style's full name.*

▶ *Since there is no Preset Manager in ImageReady, to save a library of Styles, target an empty layer so you won't make changes to your file, then delete any unwanted Styles one-by-one by selecting them in the Styles palette and clicking the "Delete style" button (the trash can) at the bottom of the palette. When you've eliminated all the Styles you don't want, click the small triangle in the upper right corner of the Styles palette and choose Save Styles from the pop-out menu.*

To complete the Photoshop part of this tutorial, change the font for the "BEYOND THE DREAM" layer. **Wow-Styles Tutorial 3.psd** shows the file at this stage.

The selected type

After editing the type

10 Adding a Rollover Style in ImageReady. In ImageReady you can use all the Styles you can use in Photoshop. And you can also take advantage of *Rollover Styles,* which have built-in interactivity.

Start up ImageReady and open the **Wow-Styles Tutorial 4.psd** file. This file is a version of the postcard file, scaled down for the Web and with button graphics added. Each oval button is on its own layer.

From the pop-out menu of ImageReady's Styles palette, choose the **Wow-20 Button Styles** and **click the Append or Replace button.** 👁 *See the tip on page 29 about choosing to append or replace Styles.*

*The **Wow-Style Tutorial 4.psd** file*

Next, in the Layers palette, **click the name of one of the button Shape layers** to target this layer; **in the Styles palette click the Wow Button 24-All Three** Style. ImageReady will apply the Style and create an interactive *slice* (the smallest area that includes the entire

button graphic and its Style elements). **Apply the same Rollover Style** to the other button graphics.

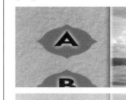

*Before (top) and after applying the **Wow Button 24-All Three** Rollover Style to one of the button layers*

As in Photoshop, you can make changes to a "styled" button: **Target a button layer, press Ctrl/⌘-T** (for Edit > Free Transform), and

*The **Wow-Styles Tutorial 4.psd** file with the **Wow Button 24-All Three** Rollover Style applied to all the buttons*

Alt/Option-drag inward on a side handle of the Transform box. (Linked buttons will be transformed together.)

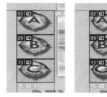

When you transform a "Rollover-styled" button, the Style and its layer-based slice will both conform to the new shape. Press the Enter key to complete the transformation.

2 Styles for Photos

In this section you'll find **One-Click Wow Styles** designed especially to enhance photos. Some of these Styles are also ideal for paintings you create using the methods described in "Section 4."

▶ *It's likely that many of the photo files that you'll want to apply a Style to will need one of the changes below:*

- *If the image is a "flattened" file—that is, it consists only of a Photoshop "Background" layer—you'll want to double-click on its name to change it to a non-Background so it can accept a Style.*

- *Many of the* **Wow Styles** *for photos create edge treatments, such as dimensional frames. Some of the effects that are built into these Styles—for instance, Drop Shadows—are designed to extend outward from the edges of the image. For these effects to show up, you'll need extra space around the edges. To add space, choose Image > Canvas Size and increase the Width and Height.*

- *Many digital photos and scanned images are stored in the compressed JPEG format. Opening and then resaving these files as JPEGs again can create an obvious reduction in photo quality. So after you edit a JPEG—by applying a Style or any other way—be sure to save it in a different (lossless) format such as the native Photoshop (.psd) format.*
  See the tip on page 26 for a discussion of file formats available in Photoshop.

Photo Gallery

On these next four pages are just a few samples of what you can do with the seven libraries of **Wow 7 Styles designed for photos.** (Pages 32–45 show examples of all of the Styles in these libraries.) For some of the images shown here, the Styles have been scaled to fit. 👁 *See "Scaling a Style" on pages 16–17 for tips on scaling.*

1 *Color FX 07* "colorizes" the photo, with the colors depending on the image. **2** *Edges 01* creates a vignette for use on a white background. **3** *Frame 04* is used here with its mat color changed, as described on page 40. **4** *Edges 08*'s negative edges conform to the content of the photo. **5** *Tint FX 03* is a "75% sepiatone"; it applies a brown tint but keeps some of the original color (compare examples 18 and 19 on page 36). **6** *Framing several photos with the same Style (here **Frame 07**) helps unify them as a group.* **7** *Dark-room 09* adds drama to clouds and sunsets by overlaying a red-to-yellow gradient. **8** *Used on this color photo, **Edges 08** inverts the color to form a custom edge.* **9** *Tint FX 06* creates a textured blue duotone effect with a soft inner edge and outer shadow.

6

7

8

9

10

Photo Gallery
continued

10 Here **Darkroom 04**'s exaggerated color makes a lively image even more so. **11 Edges 03**'s soft, dark edges, combined with the round-cornered framing, enhance the antique character of this photo. **12 Frame 05**'s dark beveled wood also adds to the antique look of this photo. **13** The lightly etched border of **Frame 09** lends the modern look of a slip-in glass frame. **14 Frame 06** creates the "retro" look of tortoiseshell Bakelite. **15 Texture 04** overlays a canvas-and-brush-stroke pattern. **16** The dark semi-transparent border in **Edges 05** provides a modern framing treatment. **17** Here **Darkroom 04** builds color (compare the exaggerated effect in 10). **18 Tint FX 01** overlays a 60% sepiatone on the original color and adds both a glow and a shadow to the edges. **19 Tint FX 09**'s sepia completely replaces the original color and also adds a canvas texture. **20 Edges 07** puts the photo under clear, polished acrylic. **21** The stippled transparent borders of **Edges 04** allow whatever is on the layers below to show through. **22 Frame 03**'s beveled molding comes with a beige mat inside the frame. (The mats for all of the **Wow 7-02 Frame Styles** can be turned on or off by setting the Inner Glow's Opacity to 100% or 0%; you can also change the Inner Glow's Size to control mat width.)

16

18

17

19

21

20

22

Photo Effects Samples

Edges

The **Wow-Edges** Layer Styles create vignettes and border treatments for photos. **Edges 06–10** include drop shadows.  **See the tips on page 40 to learn how to convert a Background so you can apply a Style, and how to add space so the drop shadow can show.**

Edges 01 creates a soft-edged vignette for a photo that will be placed on a white background. **Edges 02** desaturates and lightens the edges. **Edges 03** darkens the border. **Edges 04** dithers to transparency, so it creates a "speckled vignette" that lets the background show through regardless of its color.

Edges 05 and **06** provide two speckled framing treatments.

The highlights at the edges of **07** create the look of an image under acrylic resin. This Style can be useful as a button treatment for a photo or an icon.

In **08–10** the shape and colors of the border area will vary, depending on the photo you apply it to, because these Styles invert the colors at the edges of the image. If you turn off visibility for the drop shadow for **10,** it provides another "vignette to white" option.

Wow-Edges 01

Wow-Edges 02

Wow-Edges 03

Wow-Edges 04

Wow-Edges 05

Wow-Edges 06

Wow-Edges 07

Wow-Edges 08

Wow-Edges 09

Wow-Edges 10

Frames

With one click, each of the **Wow-Frame** Layer Styles creates a dimensional picture-frame treatment.

▶ *If you try to apply a Style to a Background layer, nothing will happen. To convert a Background to a non-Background layer that can accept a style, double-click "Background" in the Layers palette and then click OK.*

If you want to include the drop shadow that's built into these **Wow-Frame** Styles, there has to be some empty, transparent space around the image for the shadow to extend into.

▶ *To add empty space at the edges, choose Image > Canvas Size and increase the Width and Height.*

Each Style in the **Wow-Frame** set includes a "color mat" Option. Once you've applied the Style to a layer, if the mat isn't visible, you can make it appear as follows: Double-click the ƒ icon next to the layer's name in the Layers palette and when the Layer Styles dialog box opens, click "Inner Glow" in the list along the left edge; then in the Inner Glow section, change the Opacity to 100%. (You can also do the opposite—completely "turn off" a mat by setting the Opacity to 0%.) To change a mat's color, click the Inner Glow's color swatch and pick a new color.

Frame 07 and **08** are made of woven materials. **Frame 09** sandwiches an image between sheets of glass.

👁 *See the "Photo Gallery" on pages 34–37 for more description of individual **Wow-Frame** Styles.*

ORIGINAL PHOTO: © JHDAVIS DESIGN

Wow-Frame 01*

Wow-Frame 02*

Wow-Frame 03*

Wow-Frame 04*

All of the **Wow-Frame Styles include surface patterns or textures. If you need to scale one of these Styles to fit your file, there are certain scaling percentages that will ensure that the patterns stay sharp and clear.* 👁 *See "Scaling a Style" on pages 16–17 for help.*

Wow-Frame 05*

Wow-Frame 06*

Wow-Frame 07*

Wow-Frame 08*

Wow-Frame 09*

Wow-Frame 10*

Tints & Antique Effects

The **Wow-Tint FX** Styles create sepia-tone (**01–04**), black-and-white (**05**), blue tint (**06** and **07**) and antique effects (**08–10**), keeping different amounts of the original color. (Styles **02, 05, 08,** and **09** replace the original color entirely.)

All the **Wow-Tint FX** Styles except **05** include drop shadows. 👁 *See "Frames" on page 40 to learn how to add space so the drop shadow will show up.*

You can use any of the **Tint FX** series *without* the lightened or darkened edges. First apply the Style, then double-click the 𝑓 to the right of the layer's name in the Layers palette, click "Inner Glow" in the list of effects in the Layer Style dialog box, and in the Inner Glow section move the Size slider left to 0.

Tint FX 08 "antiques" an image by adding a dark edge, a slightly tinted black-and-white tone, and a "pebbled" surface.
Tint FX 09 is similar, but with a light edge and a canvas texture, and **10** has a subtler edge and a 5% contribution of the original color of the image. You can make the texture less pronounced by

ORIGINAL PHOTO: © JHDAVIS DESIGN

reducing the Depth in the Texture section, listed under "Bevel and Emboss" in the Layer Style dialog box, or by reducing the Opacity of the Pattern Overlay.

Wow-Tint FX 01

Wow-Tint FX 02

Wow-Tint FX 03

Wow-Tint FX 04

Wow-Tint FX 05

Wow-Tint FX 06

Wow-Tint FX 07

Wow-Tint FX 08*

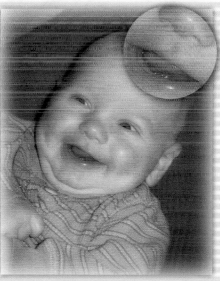

Wow-Tint FX 09*

Wow-Tint FX 10*

*Some of the **Wow-Tint FX** Styles include patterns or textures. If you need to scale one of these Styles to fit your file, there are certain scaling percentages that will ensure that the patterns stay sharp and clear.* 👁 *See "Scaling a Style" on pages 16–17 for help.*

Color Overlay Effects

The **Wow-Color FX** Styles use overlays of color—either solid colors or gradients—to create multicolor tints, changing the color of an image for practical or surreal and dramatic effects.

Styles **01** and **02** darken and lighten the image, respectively, so that the image can serve as a subtle background for light or dark type set in a layer above it.

Styles **03–07** create posterization and color-inversion special effects based on the colors in the original image.

The gradient overlays in **08–10** replace the color in the original image with multiple hues.

▶ *After you apply a **Wow-Color FX** Style to a layer, you can change the colors themselves or the angle or position of the color blend as follows: Double-click the ƒ to the right of the "styled" layer's name in the Layers palette. In the Layer Style dialog box, click on the "Color Overlay" or "Gradient Overlay" entry in the list at the left side of the dialog box, then reduce the Opacity to reduce the Overlay's contribution. For a Gradient Overlay, choose a different color combination from the pop-out Gradient palette. Change the direction of the color shift by dragging in the Angle circle, or drag in the main working window to reposition the gradient relative to the image.*

Wow-Color FX 01

Wow-Color FX 02

Wow-Color FX 03

Wow-Color FX 04

Wow-Color FX 05

Wow-Color FX 06

Wow-Color FX 07

Wow-Color FX 08

Wow-Color FX 09

Wow-Color FX 10

Darkroom & Image-Enhancing Effects

Wow-Darkroom Styles **01–03** focus attention and add subtle enhancements; **01** darkens the top and bottom, **02** darkens the top only, and **03** darkens the edges and lightens the center.*

Style **04** exaggerates the saturation (or intensity) of the colors. (It will have no effect on a black-and-white picture.)

Style **05** adds a dark edging and also *solarizes* the image, turning some colors negative and leaving others positive. To use the effect without the darkened edges, you can apply the Style, then double-click "Inner Glow" in the list of effects that appears in the Layers palette, and move the Inner Glow's Size slider to 0.

Style **06** makes a negative. And **07** converts the image to a limited range of colors; light colors turn yellow and orange, darker colors become gray.

Styles **08–10** are particularly good for enhancing sunset skies; you can move the gradients to position the colors relative to the horizon. 👁 **See the tip on page 44 for realigning a gradient.**

ORIGINAL PHOTOS: © JHDAVIS DESIGN

Wow-Darkroom 01

Wow-Darkroom 02

Wow-Darkroom 03

Wow-Darkroom 04

*Wow-Darkroom 11–15 are subtle variations on Wow-Darkroom 03.

Wow-Darkroom 05

Wow-Darkroom 06

Wow-Darkroom 07

Wow-Darkroom 08

Wow-Darkroom 09

Wow-Darkroom 10

Film Grain, Noise & Mezzotints

A pattern or texture can provide a subtle artistic treatment for a single image, or it can help to unify several photos. 👁 *See the tip on page 40 to learn how to convert a Background so you can apply a Style.*

Some of the Styles in the **Wow-Grain** set produce mezzotint-like effects, adding dots, lines, or streaks. Others (**01–03**) can simulate film grain or "digital noise." These can help hide pixel artifacts that may appear in low-resolution images or help unify photos in different layers of a collage. You can customize a **Wow-Grain** Style after you apply it by double-clicking the **ƒ** that appears to the right of the "styled" layer's name in the Layers palette, then clicking the "Pattern Overlay" entry in the list in the Layer Style dialog box. You can then Scale the grain to the size you need, or change its Opacity, or change the Blend mode—for instance, switching the Blend mode from Overlay to Soft Light will reduce the contrast of the grain.

Styles **04–06** are variations on a reticulated mezzotint effect, and **07** and **08** create irregular blotches for a freckled or dappled look.

Style **09** creates a diagonal pattern of brushed lines. And **10** creates a horizontal pattern of high-tech scan lines.

ORIGINAL PHOTO: © CORBIS IMAGES ROYALTY FREE, FOOD PERSPECTIVES

Wow-Grain 01*

Wow-Grain 02*

Wow-Grain 03*

Wow-Grain 04*

* *The names of all Styles in the **Wow-Grain** library include the * symbol, which indicates that a surface pattern or texture is part of the Style. If you need to scale one of these Styles to fit your file, there are certain scaling percentages that will ensure that the patterns stay sharp and clear.* 👁 *See "Scaling a Style" on pages 16–17 for help.*

Wow-Grain 05*

Wow-Grain 06*

Wow-Grain 07*

Wow-Grain 08*

Wow-Grain 09*

Wow-Grain 10*

Paper, Canvas & Other Texture Overlays

When you create a painting in Photoshop—whether "from scratch" or from a photo—adding the texture of paper or canvas can complete the illusion. The **Wow! Textures** can also simply be applied to a photo or graphic to add personality. 👁 *See the tip on page 40 to learn how to convert a Background so you can apply a Style.*

Wow-Texture 01 simulates watercolor paper. Style **02** is an irregularly textured canvas, **03** "bevels" any semi-transparent brush strokes you apply and adds a canvas texture as well, and **04** simulates canvas with impasto brush strokes. Style **05** simulates pebble board, **06** and **07** are rough surfaces for pastel or chalk, **08** is cracked paint, **09** simulates watercolor with salt stains, and **10** simulates the fresco effect of painting on a plastered surface.

The "painting" used in this example (a detail of which is shown below) was made from a photo by using Tool Presets from the **Wow-AH-Pastels** library, which are based on the Art History brush. 👁 *See "Media Brushes" on page 79 to find out how to use the Wow-Textures in combination with the Wow Tool Presets.*

ORIGINAL PHOTO/PAINTING
© JHDAVIS DESIGN

Wow-Texture 01*

Wow-Texture 02*

Wow-Texture 03*

Wow-Texture 04*

All of the **Wow-Texture Styles include surface patterns or textures. If you need to scale one of these Styles to fit your file, there are certain scaling percentages that will ensure that the patterns stay sharp and clear.* 👁 *"Scaling a Style" on pages 16–17 tells how.*

Wow-Texture 05*   **Wow-Texture 06***   **Wow-Texture 07***

Wow-Texture 08*   **Wow-Texture 09***   **Wow-Texture 10***

3 Styles for Type & Graphics

The Styles in this section (from **Wow 7** libraries **08–20**) were designed to add color, dimension, and material characteristics to type and graphics. Choose a Style for your project, apply it, and then tweak it if you like, as described in "Customizing Styles" on pages 18–19.

▶ *You can "combine" Styles by applying separate Styles to the layered elements of a graphic. For instance, to create the look of a carved, translucent amulet, the **Wow-Gems 19** Style was applied to a graphic on the upper layer, and the lighter **Wow-Gems 08** was applied to an oval shape on the layer below.*

When you arrive at a combination of Styles you like and you think you might want to use it again, one way to save the "combined Style" is to save (in Photoshop format) a file you've applied it to. Whenever you want to use the combination again, open this file and copy and paste the Styles, as described in "Copying & Pasting Styles" on page 20. ◉ *For other examples of "combined" Styles, see page 56.*

Type & Graphics Gallery

The next five pages show some of the "magic" you can work on graphics and type using the 12 sets of Wow Styles on pages 58–81. (Some Styles have been scaled to fit the graphics shown here.)

1, 2, 3 *Rocks 03, 04, and 05 are three different color versions of the same rough rock.* **4** *Rocks 12 is white stone* **5** *The thick gold stroke of* **Stroke 09**, *which extends outward from all the edges of this black graphic, fills in the small negative spaces, leaving transparency only in the large sun element at the bottom.* **6** **Chrome 17** *applies a dark finish with bright, raised bevels at the edges.* **7** *After* **Plastic 19** *was applied, the rainbow Gradient Overlay was repositioned to put its colors where we wanted them.* **8** *The* **Rocks 02** *Style was scaled to 25% after it was applied.* **9** *Glass 19* *makes the flat shapes and lettering of this type look like water.* **10** *Like many of the other Wow Styles designed for photos,* **Edges 05** *can work well on graphics also.*

continued on page 54

1,2,3,4

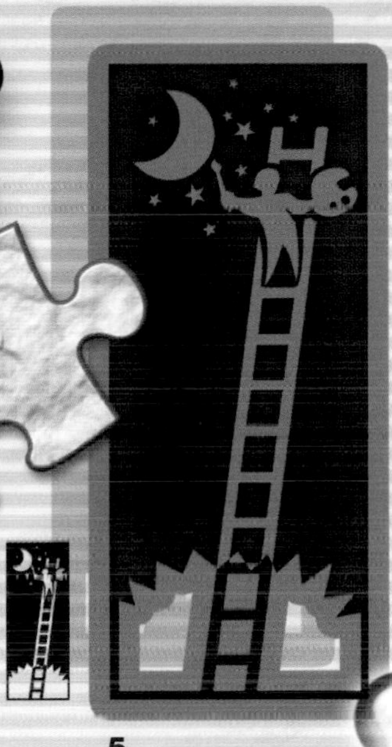

5

6

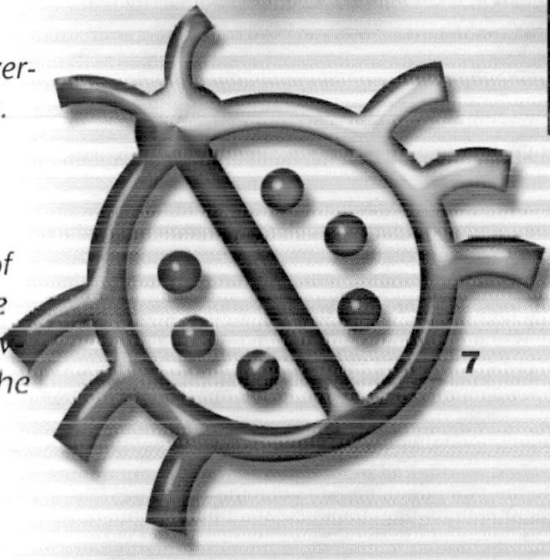

7

8

9

10

53

Type & Graphics Gallery
continued

11 *Woods 06* adds dimension and the grain and glow of smooth polished wood. **12** *Halo 13* lightens the interior, adding an overall speckle and a dark outer "halo"; like most Styles with interior edge effects, it looks different on bolder elements than on thin ones. **13** *Metals 19* simulates chiseled steel. **14** *Glow 03* and 04 turn edges into glowing neon tubes. **15** *Stroke 06* and 07 add color strokes and fills; sharp shadows add dimension. **16** *Rocks 01* creates bricks, complete with indented mortar. **17** *Gems 19* on the graphics and the lighter *Gems 08* on the oval in the layer below combine for a backlit effect. **18** *Plastic 15* creates an opaque, polished surface. **19** *Metals 15* adds the look of rusted, deeply pitted metal. **20** *Plastic 09* produces a rounded, translucent blue-green. **21** *Stroke 20* is great for "comic book" type. **22** In the Chrome set, 15 is darkest. **23** *Glass 20* produces rounded smoked glass. **24** *Organics 19* produces a rustic woven look. **25** *Halo 09* "carves" into the surface of the layers below.

continued on page 56

17

18

19

TOXIC

BEND O FLEX 20

21 "Gee whiz!"

JUST GOT BETTER The Best 22

23

24

25

Type & Graphics Gallery
continued

26 Glow 10 *turns the lines of this logo into neon tubes in the "off" state.* **27 Glow 08** *turns the neon "on."* **28 Rocks 07** *is raw Kryptonite.* **29 Plastic 05** *creates swirled color inside chrome edges.* **30 Woods 18** *produces beveled pine.* **31** *Gradient-filled* **Stroke 18** *applied to a rectangle makes a surface for* **Halo 11**, *applied to a graphic in the layer above, to "carve" into.* **32 Plastic 13** *applied to a layer above a shape treated with* **Plastic 14** *creates a stamped sign.* **33** *The bright placer gold of* **Metals 16** *on the star complements the duller bronze of* **Metals 15** *on the type.* **34 Metals 09** *produces brushed steel with polished edges.* **35 Halo 16** *adds a rainbow halo without changing the graphic's original color, here red.* **36 Organics 04** *makes a raised green edge around a woven fill.* **37 Halo 18** *makes the art disappear, leaving only a dark exterior halo.* **38 Gems 11** *produces a raised abalone texture.* **39 Chrome 13** *adds a matte finish to broad, flat areas.* **40 Plastic 08** *is a clear, rounded blue.* **41** *The boldness of each part of the graphic determines how much of* **Glow 16**'s *yellow inner glow can color the interior.*

26

27

29

28

30

31

32

33

Chromes

The Layer Styles in the **Wow-Chrome** set were designed for use on type or graphics, to simulate various kinds of reflective surfaces. The Styles are shown here applied to a file with a Resolution setting of 225 pixels/inch.

Wow-Chrome 11 is the only one of these Layer Styles that allows some of the original color of the graphic or type to come through in the chrome. So if you had started with a green symbol, for instance, instead of the gray shown here, your chrome would show a slight green tint. All other **Wow-Chrome** Styles produce the same results regardless of the starting color. 👁 *See "One-Click Wow! Quick Start" on pages 3–5 for directions for loading Styles.*

▶ *In Styles whose names include the * symbol, a built-in surface pattern or texture is used to create the illusion of the environment reflected in the chrome. If you need to scale one of these Styles to fit your file, there are certain scaling percentages that will ensure that the patterns stay sharp and clear.* 👁 *See "Scaling a Style" on pages 16–17 for help.*

Original Graphic

Wow-Chrome 01*

Wow-Chrome 02*

Wow-Chrome 03

Wow-Chrome 04

Wow-Chrome 05

Wow-Chrome 06

Wow-Chrome 07

Wow-Chrome 08

Wow-Chrome 09

Wow-Chrome 10*

Wow-Chrome 11*

Wow-Chrome 12*

Wow-Chrome 13

Wow-Chrome 14*

Wow-Chrome 15

Wow-Chrome 16*

Wow-Chrome 17*

Wow-Chrome 18

Wow-Chrome 19

Wow-Chrome 20

Metals

The Layer Styles in the **Wow-Metals** set were designed to make type or graphics look like they were stamped, chiseled, molded, or otherwise created from gold, steel, iron, or other metals, some glowing hot. Rough-surfaced Styles typically use the same pattern both in a Pattern Overlay effect and in the Texture aspect of the Bevel And Emboss effect. The results shown here were achieved by applying each of the Styles to a file with a Resolution setting of 225 pixels/inch.

👁 *See "One-Click Wow! Quick Start," pages 3–5 for directions for loading Styles.*

👁 *See "Scaling a Style," pages 16–17 to learn about the relationship between Layer Styles and the Resolution setting in the Image Size dialog box.*

▶ *Styles whose names include the * symbol have a built-in surface pattern or texture. If you need to scale one of these Styles to fit your file, there are certain scaling percentages that will ensure that the patterns stay sharp and clear. See "Scaling a Style," pages 16–17.*

Original Graphic

Wow-Metals 01*

Wow-Metals 02*

Wow-Metals 03*

Wow-Metals 04*

Wow-Metals 05*

Wow-Metals 06*

Wow-Metals 07*

Wow-Metals 08*

Wow-Metals 09*   **Wow-Metals 10***   **Wow-Metals 11***   **Wow-Metals 12***

Wow-Metals 13*   **Wow-Metals 14***   **Wow-Metals 15***   **Wow-Metals 16***

Wow-Metals 17   **Wow-Metals 18**   **Wow-Metals 19***   **Wow-Metals 20**

Glass, Ice & Crystal

The Layer Styles in the **Wow-Glass** set were designed to make type or graphics look as if they were formed of transparent crystalline materials. Some of them also feature highly reflective textured surfaces.

The **Wow-Glass** Styles completely remove or replace the original color of the graphic, so that no matter what color it was to start with, the original color is not evident in the "styled" element.

The effects shown here are the results of applying the **Wow-Glass** Styles to a file with a Resolution setting of 225 pixels/inch. *See "Scaling a Style" on pages 16–17 to learn about the relationship between Layer Styles and the Resolution setting.*

*Styles whose names include the * symbol have a built-in surface pattern or texture. If you need to scale one of these Styles to fit your file, there are certain scaling percentages that will ensure that the patterns stay sharp and clear. See "Scaling a Style," pages 16–17.

Original Graphic **Wow-Glass 01** **Wow-Glass 02**

Wow-Glass 03* **Wow-Glass 04** **Wow-Glass 05***

Wow-Glass 06 **Wow-Glass 07** **Wow-Glass 08**

Wow-Glass 09

Wow-Glass 10*

Wow-Glass 11

Wow-Glass 12

Wow-Glass 13*

Wow-Glass 14*

Wow-Glass 15

Wow-Glass 16

Wow-Glass 17

Wow-Glass 18*

Wow-Glass 19

Wow-Glass 20*

Gems & Smooth Stones

The Layer Styles in the **Wow-Gems** set were designed to endow type or graphics with the colorful brilliance of polished gems, amber, or shells, as well as marble and other kinds of stone, with accompanying translucency and reflectivity.

All of the **Wow-Gems** Styles apply surface patterning, and one (**Wow-Gems 11**) has a bumpy surface texture as well.

The effects shown here are the results of applying the **Wow-Gems** Styles to a file with a Resolution setting of 225 pixels/inch. 👁 *See "Scaling a Style" on pages 10–11 for the relationship between Layer Styles and the Resolution setting.*

*The names of all the Styles in the Wow-Gems set include the * symbol, which indicates that a surface pattern or texture is part of the Style. If you need to scale one of these Styles to fit your file, there are certain scaling percentages that will ensure that the patterns stay sharp and clear. 👁 See "Scaling a Style" on pages 16–17.*

Original Graphic

Wow-Gems 01*

Wow-Gems 02*

Wow-Gems 03*

Wow-Gems 04*

Wow-Gems 05*

Wow-Gems 06*

Wow-Gems 07*

Wow-Gems 08*

Wow-Gems 09*

Wow-Gems 10*

Wow-Gems 11*

Wow-Gems 12*

Wow-Gems 13*

Wow-Gems 14*

Wow-Gems 15*

Wow-Gems 16*

Wow-Gems 17*

Wow-Gems 18*

Wow-Gems 19*

Wow-Gems 20*

Plastics

The Styles in the **Wow-Plastics** set imitate various kinds of plastics, some opaque and others translucent. The colors are integrated into the Styles, so the original color of the type or graphic doesn't affect the final result. Most of the **Wow-Plastics** are smooth-surfaced, but four (**03, 13, 14** and **18**) are textured.

Wow-Plastics 13 and **14** are designed to work together to create the look of a sign or license plate—the black is applied to a layer with graphics or type, and the yellow is applied to the larger shape of the sign or plate in the layer underneath. 👁 *See "Type & Graphics Gallery" on page 53 for a layered sign example.*

The effects shown here are the results of applying the Styles to a file with a Resolution of 225 pixels/inch.

* Styles whose names include the * symbol have a built-in surface pattern or texture. If you need to scale one of these Styles to fit your file, there are certain scaling percentages that will ensure that the patterns stay sharp and clear. 👁 *See "Scaling a Style" on pages 16–17.*

Original Graphic

Wow-Plastic 01

Wow-Plastic 02

Wow-Plastic 03*

Wow-Plastic 04

Wow-Plastic 05 *

Wow-Plastic 06

Wow-Plastic 07

Wow-Plastic 08

Wow-Plastic 09

Wow-Plastic 10

Wow-Plastic 11

Wow-Plastic 12

Wow-Plastic 13 *

Wow-Plastic 14 *

Wow-Plastic 15

Wow-Plastic 16

Wow-Plastic 17

Wow-Plastic 18 *

Wow-Plastic 19

Wow-Plastic 20

Polished & Textured Woods

The Layer Styles in the **Wow-Woods** set provide the look of wood—common or exotic, raw or polished, or even encased in resin. In some the wood surfaces are smooth, while in others the grain is raised.

After you've applied a **Wow-Woods** Style, you can change the drop shadow by double-clicking the icon beside the layer's name in the Layers palette, then clicking on Drop Shadow in the list of effects in the Layer Style dialog box and adjusting the shadow parameters. 👁 *See "Scaling a Style" on pages 16–17 for the relationship between Layer Styles and the Resolution setting.*

** The names of all the Styles in the Wow-Woods set include the * symbol, which indicates that a surface pattern or texture is part of the Style. If you need to scale one of these Styles to fit your file, there are certain scaling percentages that will ensure that the patterns stay sharp and clear. 👁 See "Scaling a Style" on pages 16–17.*

Original Graphic

Wow-Woods 01*

Wow-Woods 02*

Wow-Woods 03*

Wow-Woods 04*

Wow-Woods 05*

Wow-Woods 06*

Wow-Woods 07*

Wow-Woods 08*

Wow-Woods 09*

Wow-Woods 10*

Wow-Woods 11*

Wow-Woods 12*

Wow-Woods 13*

Wow-Woods 14*

Wow-Woods 15*

Wow-Woods 16*

Wow-Woods 17*

Wow-Woods 18*

Wow-Woods 19*

Wow-Woods 20*

Rock, Brick & Other Materials

The Layer Styles in the **Wow-Rocks** set were designed to endow type and graphics with the textures of everything from alien minerals (**07** is molten Kryptonite) to a variety of building materials—from bricks (**01**) to rough and smooth stone (including sandstone, **20**), and even various kinds of weathered ores (**11, 13, 16,** and **19**).

The effects shown here are the results of applying the Styles to a file with a Resolution setting of 225 pixels/inch. 👁 *See "Scaling a Style" on pages 16–17 for the relationship between Layer Styles and the Resolution setting.*

* *The names of all the Styles in the Wow-Rocks set include the * symbol, which indicates that a surface pattern or texture is part of the Style. If you need to scale one of these Styles to fit your file, there are certain scaling percentages that will ensure that the patterns stay sharp and clear.* 👁 *See "Scaling a Style" on pages 16–17.*

Original Graphic

Wow-Rocks 01*

Wow-Rocks 02*

Wow-Rocks 03*

Wow-Rocks 04*

Wow-Rocks 05*

Wow-Rocks 06*

Wow-Rocks 07*

Wow-Rocks 08*

Wow-Rocks 09*

Wow-Rocks 10*

Wow-Rocks 11*

Wow-Rocks 12*

Wow-Rocks 13*

Wow-Rocks 14*

Wow-Rocks 15*

Wow-Rocks 16*

Wow-Rocks 17*

Wow-Rocks 18*

Wow-Rocks 19*

Wow-Rocks 20*

Organic Patterns

The Layer Styles in the **Wow-Organics** are seamlessly wrapping photographic patterns and textures, great for backgrounds, panels, or special fills for display text or graphics. Most of the **Wow-Organics** have shadows, bevels, or subtly embossed surface textures, so these Styles can be used to turn type or graphics into dimensional objects. But these attributes can also be turned off when you simply want a background or fill. 👁 *See the tip on page 74 for changing or removing individual effects from a Style.*

The relatively large and detailed **00–03** are designed for backgrounds.

▶ *With the Pattern Overlay section of the Layer Style dialog box open, you can drag in the main image window to shift the pattern. This is especially useful for repositioning large patterns.*

Organics 04 and **05** include stroked edges and inner shadows that make them ideal for type. Style **06** shows the brush work of coarse stucco. Styles **07, 08,** and **17–20** are woven materials whose patterns are enhanced with texture. Organics **09–12** are papers, **13** is a corroded surface with stark outlining, **14** is cork, and **15** and **16** are bamboo variations.

Wow-Organics 00*

Wow-Organics 01*

Wow-Organics 02*

Wow-Organics 03*

Wow-Organics 04*

Wow-Organics 05*

Wow-Organics 06*   **Wow-Organics 07***   **Wow-Organics 08***

*The names of all the **Wow-Organics** Styles include the * symbol, indicating a built-in surface pattern or texture. If you need to scale one of these Styles to fit your file, there are certain scaling percentages that will ensure that the patterns stay sharp and clear. 👁 See "Scaling a Style" on pages 16–17.*

Wow-Organics 09*

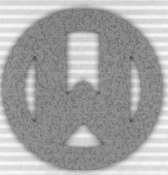

Wow-Organics 10*

Wow-Organics 11*

Wow-Organics 12*

Wow-Organics 13*

Wow-Organics 14*

Wow-Organics 15*

Wow-Organics 16*

Wow-Organics 17*

Wow-Organics 18*

Wow-Organics 19*

Wow-Organics 20*

Patterns & Fabrics

The Layer Styles in the **Wow-Fabric** library are seamlessly repeating patterns. The patterns are also subtly embossed on the surface, the edges are beveled, and drop shadows have been added so that these Styles can be used to turn type or graphics into dimensional objects. But these attributes can also be turned off if what you need is simply a pattern to use as a background or fill.

▶ *To change or remove any of the individual effects in a Style you've applied, simply double-click the ƒ icon for the "styled" layer in the Layers palette, then find the specific effect in the list in the Layer Style dialog box. You can "uncheck" the effect—for example, click on the check mark to the left of "Drop Shadow," "Bevel and Emboss" or "Texture" in the list. Or click the name of the effect and change the settings to taste.*

▶ *The 21 Patterns used in the **Wow-Fabric** Styles plus 24 more Patterns can be found in the **Wow 7-Fabric Patterns** library.*

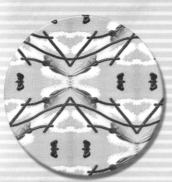

Wow-Fabric 00 *

Wow-Fabric 01 *

Wow-Fabric 02 *

Wow-Fabric 03 *

Wow-Fabric 04 *

Wow-Fabric 05 *

Wow-Fabric 06 *   **Wow-Fabric 07 ***   **Wow-Fabric 08 ***

** The names of all the Styles in the **Wow-Fabric** library include the * symbol, which indicates that a pattern is part of the Style. If you need to scale one of these Styles to fit your file, there are certain scaling percentages that will ensure that the patterns stay sharp and clear.* 👁 *See "Scaling a Style" on pages 16–17.*

Wow-Fabric 09 *

Wow-Fabric 10 *

Wow-Fabric 11 *

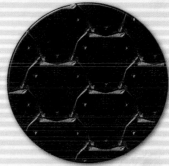

Wow-Fabric 12 *

Wow-Fabric 13 *

Wow-Fabric 14 *

Wow-Fabric 15 *

Wow-Fabric 16 *

Wow-Fabric 17 *

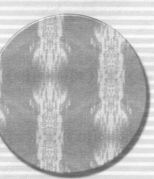

Wow-Fabric 18 *

Wow-Fabric 19 *

Wow-Fabric 20 *

Strokes & Fills

The Layer Styles in the **Wow-Stroke** library provide everything from a simple out-line, to beveled edging with a color fill, to fill treatments that look abstract or hand-painted. Some have drop shadows to "pop" the type or graphic off the page.

▶ *To change or remove any of the individual effects in a Style you've applied, simply double-click the ƒ icon for the "styled" layer in the Lay-ers palette, then find the specific effect in the list in the Layer Style dialog box. Either "uncheck" the effect—for example, click on the check mark to the left of "Drop Shadow" in the list. Or click the name of the effect and change the settings.*

Styles **02, 04,** and **05** use the color of the original graphic.

Styles **03** and **18–20** can make great "comic book" headlines. Styles **09–15** pro-vide more sophisticated colors as well as subtle interior "ha-los," textures and gradients.

Stroke **16's** "watercolor" fill can enhance calligraphy or rough graphics. And the "crayon rubbing" fill of **17** follows the contours of the type or graphic.

Original Graphic	Wow-Stroke 01*	Wow-Stroke 02
Wow-Stroke 03	Wow-Stroke 04	Wow-Stroke 05
Wow-Stroke 06	Wow-Stroke 07	Wow-Stroke 08

* Styles whose names include the * symbol have a built-in surface pattern or texture. If you need to scale one of these Styles to fit your file, there are certain scaling percentages that will ensure that the patterns stay sharp and clear. 👁 *See "Scaling a Style" on pages 16–17.*

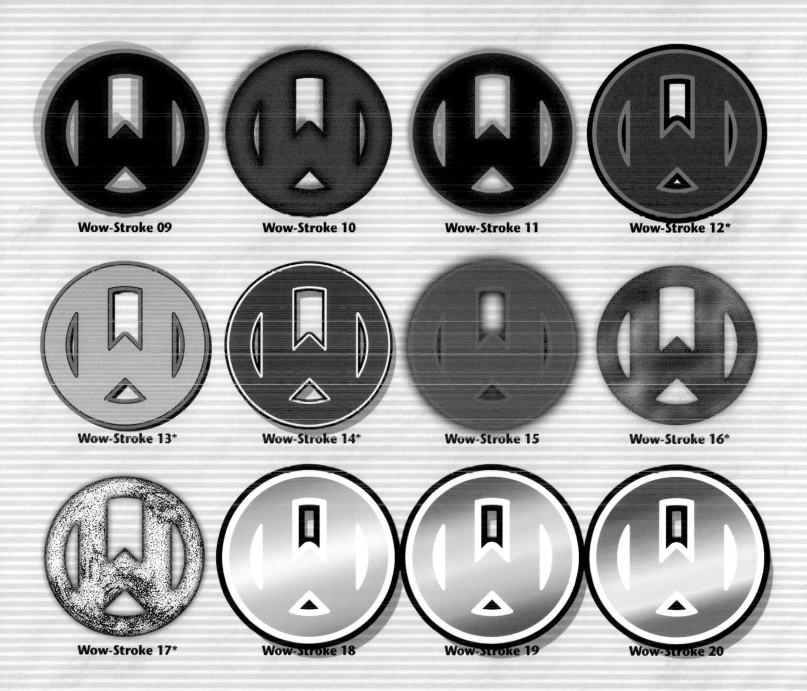

Wow-Stroke 09

Wow-Stroke 10

Wow-Stroke 11

Wow-Stroke 12*

Wow-Stroke 13*

Wow-Stroke 14*

Wow-Stroke 15

Wow-Stroke 16*

Wow-Stroke 17*

Wow-Stroke 18

Wow-Stroke 19

Wow-Stroke 20

Shadows, Halos & Embossing

Many of the **Wow-Halo** Styles are "positive and negative" pairs. So you'll find, side by side on these pages, two versions of the same general Style—one dark and one light, or one raised above the surface and one impressed into it. Shown here are the results of applying the Styles to a file with a Resolution setting of 225 pixels/inch.

The simple halos (**03** and **04**) and the rainbow Styles (**15** and **16**) keep the original fill color (here 50% gray). (The rainbows work well against "middle-tone" backgrounds rather than pure black or white.) The "noisy" halos (**05** and **06** as well as **13** and **14**) replace the original color with black and white. In all the other **Wow-Halos** the original type or graphic disappears, and the shape is defined by the halo, shadow, or embossed edge.

Styles **09** and **10** are sharp-edged and rounded versions of carved effects. **Halo 11** is a sharply embossed stamp effect, and **Halo 12** is a subtle raised emboss treatment.

Original Graphic   Wow-Halo 01   Wow-Halo 02

Wow-Halo 03   Wow-Halo 04   Wow-Halo 05

Wow-Halo 06   Wow-Halo 07   Wow-Halo 08

Wow-Halo 09

Wow-Halo 10

Wow-Halo 11

Wow-Halo 12

Wow-Halo 13

Wow-Halo 14

Wow-Halo 15

Wow-Halo 16

Wow-Halo 17

Wow-Halo 18

Wow-Halo 19

Wow-Halo 20

Glows & Neons

Most of the **Wow-Glows** work best when you apply them to type or graphics used against dark or middle-tone backgrounds that contrast with their glowing light. Shown here are the results of applying the Styles to a file with a Resolution setting of 225 pixels/inch.

The multicolor glows (**18–20**) keep the original fill color of the graphic, while all the other **Wow-Glows** Styles replace the original color with the colors shown here.

Styles **03–05** are the "off" versions of the "lit" neons created by **06–08**. In these and other neons (**10–12** and **17**), the fill of the type or graphic is eliminated, and the edges are traced with "neon tubes."

You can use **Glows 09** to turn type and graphics into a glowing "plasma field," or **13–16** to make them "burn."

Original Graphic

Wow-Glows 01

Wow-Glows 02

Wow-Glows 03

Wow-Glows 04

Wow-Glows 05

Wow-Glows 06

Wow-Glows 07

Wow-Glows 08

Wow-Glows 09

Wow-Glows 10

Wow-Glows 11

Wow-Glows 12

Wow-Glows 13

Wow-Glows 14

Wow-Glows 15

Wow-Glows 16

Wow-Glows 17

Wow-Glows 18

Wow-Glows 19

Wow-Glows 20

Button Rollover Styles

The **Wow-Button** Styles were designed to look good when applied to small on-screen navigational elements created at 72 pixels/inch. As shown in the palette below, the **Wow 7–20 Button Styles. asl** file is made up of sets of three individual Styles designed specifically for the **Normal, Over,** and **Down** states of buttons, as well as a fourth **All Three** Style. The **Normal, Over,** and **Down** Styles (shown here left-to-right) don't have built-in rollover properties. You can use them individually in Photoshop or ImageReady. But the **All Three** Styles include the JavaScript for interactivity. In ImageReady, if you apply an **All Three** Style to a button graphic, the button will change in response to what the user does with the cursor.

👁 *See "Working with Styles in Imag-eReady" on page 23 for more about Rollover Styles.*

The top three rows of Styles in each column (**01–03, 11–13, 21–23, 31–33,** and **41–43**) are color variations of five basic Styles.

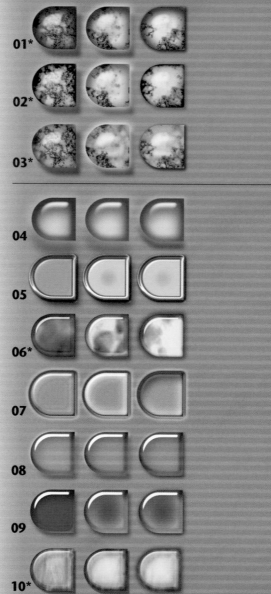

Most of the **Wow-Button** Styles replace the original color. But Style **09** retains the underlying color of the graphic or photo.

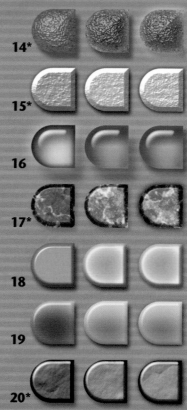

*Styles whose names include the * symbol have a built-in surface pattern or texture. If you need to scale one of these Styles to fit your file, there are certain scaling percentages that will ensure that the patterns stay sharp and clear.*
👁 *See "Scaling a Style" on pages 16–17.*

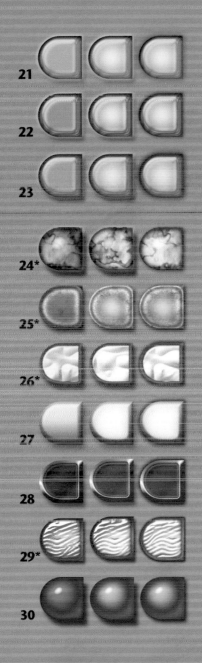

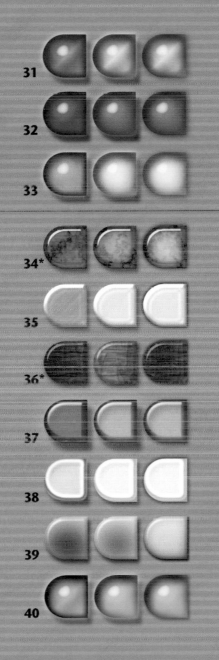

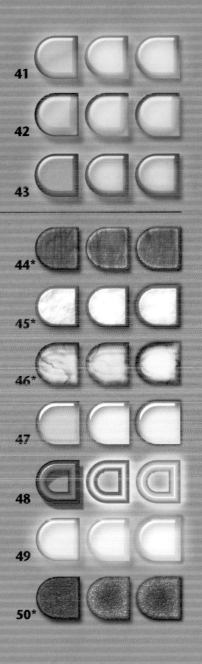

21
22
23
24*
25*
26*
27
28
29*
30

31
32
33
34*
35
36*
37
38
39
40

41
42
43
44*
45*
46*
47
48
49
50*

4 Other Wow! Presets

The world of **One-Click Wow!** holds a lot more than just Styles—from painting to retouching to elegant framing effects, all done with Presets. If you followed the instructions in steps 1 and 2 on page 3, you'll find these **Wow Presets** in your Photoshop menus:

• In the pop-out menu of the **Tool Presets** palette (found at the far left end of the Options bar) are the brand-new **Wow Custom Shape Overlays** for creating elegant "ghosted" panels to use as backdrops for text on top of your photographs, or for crafting custom frames and vignetting effects to complement your masterpieces. Also in the **Tool Presets** palette are all the **Wow-Art History Brushes**, **Wow-Pattern Stamp Brushes**, and **Wow-Art Media Brushes**, with more than 60 tools for simulating traditional artists' media, including Pastel, Chalk, Oil, Watercolor, Sponge, Stipple, and Dry Brush. See pages 93–95 and 100–101 for instructions and samples of these Presets for the Pattern Stamp, Art History Brush, and Brush. Also find a gallery of examples on pages 98–99.

• Also available in the **Tool Presets** palette's menu are the **Wow-Image Fix Brushes,** Presets for the Brush tool for whitening eyes and teeth, and neutralizing redness on the skin. See "Using the Wow! Image Fix Brushes" on page 104 for pointers.

• Finally, **Wow Presets** for the Rectangular **Marquee Tool** and **Crop Tool** will help you make selections at many popular sizes and crop images to those dimensions.

• The **Wow-Actions** for production shortcuts, enhancing paintings, photos, and graphics, and fixing images are covered on pages 105–107.

• There are **Wow-Patterns** for printed Fabric, Marble, Media substrates, Miscellaneous Surfaces, Noise (which can be used for artistic treatments or to simulate film grain), and Organic materials such as wood and woven fibers. The **Wow-Patterns** will be available from the pop-out menu anywhere the Patterns palette appears, for instance, in the Fill dialog box, in the Pattern Fill dialog box or in certain Style components that use Patterns (such as the Pattern Overlay, the Stroke, and the Texture "subeffect" of Bevel And Emboss).

• Using the **Wow-Gradients** is described on page 108.

How to Use the Wow Custom Shape Overlays

Create sophisticated "ghosted back" panels for text displayed on top of photographs, or craft custom frames and vignetting effects with Wow Custom Shape Overlays.

By combining the power and flexibility of Photoshop's Custom Shape tools (ones that use scalable geometric *shapes* rather than the *pixels* that make up the photos you are used to) with the scalable capabilities of Wow Layer Styles, you're able to quickly and efficiently create some very impressive supporting graphics.

Before you start, be sure the **Wow Presets** have been installed.
👁 *See page 3 for instructions.*

1 Choose the Custom Shape Tool which is sometimes hidden under the Rectangle Tool. All of the **Wow Custom Shape Overlays** can only be found in the Tool Preset Picker if this tool is currently active.

To access the Custom Shape Tool, click and hold the Rectangle tool in Photoshop's general Tools palette.

2 Choose the Wow-Custom Shape Overlays from the Tools Preset Picker, found in the far left of the Options bar. Select them from the pop-out menu in the upper right of the Shapes Palette in the Options bar. For creating a text panel, choose the **Wow-Panel Shape** from the bottom of the list.

To load the **Wow-Custom Shape Overlays,** select them from the pop-out menu in the upper right of the Tool Preset Picker in the Options bar.

3 Drag out your Shape and the built-in **Wow Styles** will automatically add all the tinting effects (including the semi-transparency, subtle glows, and inner halos). For our text panel here we chose the Wow-Panel Ghosted Black preset. If you want to scale or reposition the graphic, press ⌘/**Ctrl-T**, for Free Transform, and drag away to your heart's content. Since both the Shape and the assigned Style are not made up of pixels (they are "resolution independent" graphics), they will maintain their quality, no matter how you scale them!

5 Add your type. Now you can switch to the Type Tool and drag out a rectangle for your block of text, then start writing. You can change the font, size, and color from within the Options bar.

Add text to finish off your creation.

Overlay Shapes & Styles Gallery

On these pages are some examples of how you might use the **Wow-Custom Shape Overlay** presets.

▶ *To learn how to use all these custom tool presets, please read pages 84-92 before starting.*

1 *The* **Wow-Brush Clipping Mask-Sepia** *(and the* **Wow-Brush Clipping Mask-Color 6**, *and Gray version) "cuts out" your photograph by you moving the layer that holds the* **Wow-Custom Shape Overlay** *(once you've dragged it out to the desired size on your canvas) BELOW your photograph layer and pressing ⌘-Opt-G (Mac) or Ctrl-Alt-G (Windows).* **2** *Using the* **Wow-Panel Ghosted Black Custom Shape Overlay.* **3** *The* **Wow-Panel Raised Light** *preset,* **4** *The* **Wow-Square-Desaturate** *preset,* **5** *The* **Wow-Square-Ghosted Black**, **7** *The* **Wow-Brush-Ghosted White**, **8** **Wow-Panel-Ghosted White**, **9** *and* **Wow-Oval-Vignette White Ghosted** *presets.*

▶ *If your photograph is the Background layer, you can double-click its name in the Layers palette to rename it and unlock it, so it can be moved up in the layer's stack.*

5

6

7

8

9

Text Panel Overlay Variations

The **Wow Custom Shape Overlays** presets shown here were designed specifically to work as panels or backdrops for text, though you can see in the tip to the right that they can also be used to turn any background photo or graphic into a ghosted backdrop for a quick and easy collage.

T-B: Top to Bottom
B-T: Bottom to Top
L-R: Left to Right
R-L: Right to Left

Panel-Ghosted White

Panel-Ghosted Black

Panel-Raised Light

Panel-Ghosted White

Panel-Ghosted Black

Panel-Recessed Dark

**Panel-Gradient
Desaturate T-B**

**Panel-Gradient
Desaturate B-T**

**Panel-Gradient L-R
White**

Panels as Backdrops

▶ *In the two samples below, we used the **Wow-Panel-Ghosted White** preset and covered the entire background with the panel. Next, a second image was placed on a layer above and a simple Drop Shadow Layer Style was added. This method can be used for multiple Images **A** or for a close-up of a single image **B**.*

A

B

**Panel-Gradient
Desaturate L-R**

**Panel-Gradient
Desaturate R-L**

**Panel-Gradient T-B
Black**

**Panel-Gradient B-T
Black**

**Panel-Gradient T-B
White**

**Panel-Gradient B-T
White**

**Panel-Gradient L-R
Black**

**Panel-Gradient R-L
Black**

Oval Frame Variations

The Wow Custom Shape Overlay frame presets are based on rectangular shapes that have various "holes" (ovals, squares, or brush edges) punched into the centers of those shapes, thus allowing the unaltered image to show through the middle. These customized shapes have embedded **Wow Layer Styles** that create the Desaturating, Ghosting, and Vignetting effects.

Using the Wow Custom Shape Overlays designed for Framing:

▶ Once you have selected the Shape you want to use and applied the desired Wow Overlay Style in the Options bar, zoom out so you can see plenty of gray area around your image. Now, with the Custom Shape Tool active, click in the gray area above and to the left of your photograph **A** and drag down past the lower right of your image **B**, trying to center the inner shape (the oval, square, or brush edge) in your file. Without releasing the mouse

continued...

Wow-Oval-Desaturate

Wow-Oval-Ghosted White

Wow-Oval-Ghosted Black

Wow-Oval-Vignette Black

Wow-Oval-Vignette Desaturate

Wow-Oval-Vignette Ghosted Black

Wow-Oval-Vignette White

Wow-Oval-Vignette Ghosted White

button, adjust the position of the entire shape while you are drawing it out by holding down the spacebar. You can go back and forth between scaling the shape (by dragging) and repositioning it (pressing the spacebar while dragging) as many times as necessary until you achieve the size and position you like best **C**. Release the mouse button to complete the stylized shape **D**.

Square Frame Variations

▶ *You may reshape the result-ing Shape Layer by pressing ⌘/Ctrl-T and Free Transform-ing it to better fit your photo.*

Wow-Square-Desaturate

Wow-Square-Ghosted Black

Wow-Square-Ghosted White

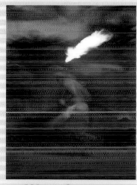
Wow-Square-Vignette Black

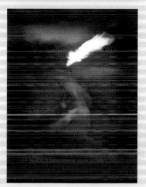
Wow-Square-Vignette Desaturate

Wow-Square-Vignette Ghosted Black

Wow-Square-Vignette White

Wow-Square-Vignette Ghosted White

Brush Frame Variations

▶ *The vector-based edge used for the **Brush** Custom Shapes is very detailed and complex and might cause your screen redraw to slow down. Be patient and we're sure you'll find it worth the extra time.*

Scaling Effects

*The tool presets are optimized for images that have a resolution of 225 pixels per inch. If the size of drop shadows, glows, and other effects overwhelm your image, you can scale the Style itself by **choosing Layer Style > Scale Effects** from the Layer menu. And as with all layers, you can control its opacity percentage in the upper left of the Layers palette. If you only want to change one component of a Layer Style, try double-clicking on the Layer Style icon on the right side of the active layer and change just the specific settings. In the image to the immediate right, we used the **Wow-Brush-Desaturate** preset to add the frame effect, then scaled the Shadow effect to make sure that it didn't dominate the image.*

Wow-Brush-Desaturate

Wow-Brush-Ghosted Black

Wow-Brush-Ghosted White

Wow-Brush-Vignette Black

Wow-Brush-Vignette Desaturate

Wow-Brush-Vignette Ghosted Black

Wow-Brush-Vignette White

Wow-Brush-Vignette Ghosted White

How to Paint with the Wow! Paint & Clone Presets

*Turn an existing photo into a painting with the **Wow-Pattern Stamp** or **Wow-Art History** Brushes. Or, start with a blank canvas and paint from scratch with the **Wow-Art Media** Brushes. All three types of brushes have matching brush tips, so you can switch back and forth seamlessly between the three painting methods.*

There are two kinds of Wow cloning brushes—the Pattern Stamp (**PS**) Presets that pull color from a source image as you paint stroke-by-stroke, and the Art History Brush (**AH**) Presets that automatically follow the color and contrast in the source image to create brush strokes. With either of these kinds of tools, you can turn a photo into a painting in five easy-to-understand steps. This process is described first for the **Wow-Pattern Stamp Brushes**, and then (on page 95) for the **Wow-Art History Brushes**. Before you start, be sure the **Wow-Tools, Wow-Photoshop Actions,** and **Wow-Styles** folders have been installed. ⊙ **See step 1 on page 3 if you need instructions.**

1 Prepare the photo. Choose the photo you want to turn into a painting. Save a copy of the file (**File > Save As** under a new name) so you'll have the original if you need to go back to it.

*This landscape was chosen as the basis for the cloned painting to be made with **Wow-PS Watercolor** brushes.*

Then make any changes that you like to the copy. For instance:

- Exaggerate its color and contrast until you have the colors you want in your painting.

After the image was cropped, the contrast was increased and the color exaggerated using Levels and Hue/Saturation adjustments.

- If you want your painting to have an "unfinished edges" look, make a selection of the edges and fill it with white. ⊙ **See pages 98–99 for several examples of paintings done this way.**

2 Load "paint" into the brush. To make the image the source for painting with the **Wow-PS** Presets, define it as a Pattern by choosing Edit > Define Pattern; everything that's visible will become a Pattern tile.

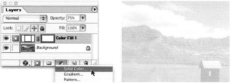

In the Pattern Name dialog box, type in a name and click OK.

Now make this new Pattern the cloning source for the painting: **Choose the Pattern Stamp** from the Tools palette and **choose your new pattern** from the pop-out menu of Pattern swatches in the tool's Options bar.

Choosing the Pattern Stamp, it shares a space with the Clone Stamp.

Clicking the little arrow to the right of the Pattern swatch in the Options bar opens the palette of samples so you can choose the Pattern you defined.

3 Make a "canvas"/surface layer. Adding a surface layer above your image makes a foundation for your painting and serves as a visual barrier between your original image and the painting layer, so you'll be able to see your brush strokes clearly as your painting develops. Click the "Create new fill or adjustment layer" button at the bottom of the Layers palette, choose Solid Color, and pick white. When the new layer appears in the Layers palette, reduce its Opacity.

With a Color Fill layer added and its Opacity reduced, you can see your photo.

▶ *Using a Wacom pressure-sensitive tablet and stylus with the **Wow Art Media, Art History and Pattern Stamp Brush Tool Presets** gives you much better control than using a mouse.* 👁 *See the tip on page 95 to compare. But even if you use a mouse, you can vary the size of the brush tip by keeping your fingers on the bracket keys and toggling the brush size up and down.*

Tapping the [key makes a brush tip smaller; tapping] enlarges the brush tip.

▶ *Be sure to take advantage of the three to five sizes of each kind of brush provided in the **Wow-Pattern Stamp** brushes, **Wow-Art History** brushes, and **Wow-Art Media** brushes. Even though you can change brush tip size by using the bracket keys, you'll get much better-looking brush strokes if you start with the brush that's closest to the size you want and then enlarge or reduce it slightly with the bracket keys.*

4 Prepare a paint layer and painting.

Click the "Create a new layer" button at the bottom of the Layers palette to add a transparent layer for painting. Then, with the Pattern Stamp still chosen (from step 2), in the Tool Presets palette choose one of the **Wow-PS** Presets; the **Wow-PS Watercolor** brushes were used for this example.

*Each type of **Wow-PS** brush is provided in at least three sizes so you can find the one that best matches the level of detail you want at any point in your painting.*

Now paint, keeping these pointers in mind:
• In general, start with a larger brush and move to smaller ones as you add finer details.
• Try to paint each differently colored area separately.
• Don't "scrub" over the image, but instead make brush strokes that follow the color and shape contours.

From time to time, increase the Opacity of the Color Fill layer to hide the original image so you can see how the painting is developing.

Viewing the painting in progress, with the Opacity of the Color Fill layer at 75% (left) and at 100% (right)

After you've used cloning brushes to create the painting, you may want to use a matching (non-cloning) **Wow-Art Media Brushes** Preset with the Brush tool and a very small brush tip, for full control as you paint the finest details. Choose colors for the Brush by Alt/Option-clicking in your paint layer.

5 Enhance the painting.
When the painting is complete, you may want to try one of these techniques to add to it:

• Increase the density of the color by making a copy of the paint layer (target the paint layer by clicking its name in the Layers palette, then press Ctrl/⌘-J to copy it). This extra layer will build up any strokes that are partially transparent, to intensify the color. If you like the result, with the duplicate (top) paint layer active, press Ctrl/⌘-E to merge the two layers together.

*The **Wow-PS Watercolor** painting with all brush strokes completed (left) and after building up the color by duplicating the paint layer (right)*

• Target the paint layer in the Layers palette and run one of the **Wow-Paint Edge Enhance** Actions by clicking on it in the Actions palette.

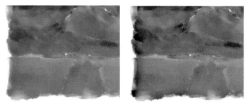

*Before (left) and after running the **Wow-Paint Edge Enhance-Subtle** Action*

▶ *The **Wow-Art Media Brushes** Presets were designed for creating paintings of your own, without cloning a photo. (The names of these Presets start with "BT," which stands for "Brush Tool," which is the tool you choose in the Tools palette in order to work with these Presets chosen from the Tool Presets palette.) Of course, these brushes can also be used for adding the finishing touches to a cloned painting as well. Strokes made with the **Wow-BT** brushes are shown below.*

Wow-BT Chalk

Wow-BT Dry Brush

Wow-BT Oil

Wow-BT Pastel

Wow-BT Sponge

Wow-BT Stipple

Wow-BT Watercolor

*Strokes painted with the seven kinds of **Wow-Art Media Brushes**. In each case the top stroke was produced with the mouse and the bottom one with a Wacom Intuos tablet.*

*The **Wow-Paint Edge Enhance Actions** work by filtering a copy of the paint layer and using Blend Modes to combine it with what's below.*

- Painting with the **Wow Presets** creates canvas or paper texture as well as brush strokes. You can make these more apparent by applying one of the **Wow-Texture Styles** to the paint layers. See examples of the **Wow-Textures** on pages 50–51.

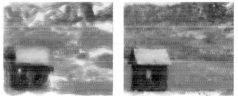

*Applying **Wow-Texture 01** to the painting layer*

To paint with the Wow-Art History Brush Presets, use this five-step process:

1 Prepare the photo. Use the same procedure described in step 1 on page 93.

2 Load "paint" into the brush. To define your photo as the source, open the History palette (**choose Window > History**) and **choose New Snapshot** from the menu that pops out from the upper-right corner of the palette; choose **Merged Layers** from the popout menu in the New Snapshot dialog box.

*Making a "Merged Layers" Snapshot of your enhanced photo, to act as a source for the **Wow-AH** brushes.*

In the History palette, **click in the column to the left of the Snapshot** you just made;

this sets it as the source for painting. Then **choose the Art History Brush from the Tools palette**, and **choose one of the Wow-AH brushes from the Tool Presets palette**.

Defining your Merged Snapshot as the source

The Art History Brush shares a spot with the History Brush.

3 Make a "canvas" layer. Use the same procedure described in step 3 on page 93.

4 Prepare a paint layer and paint. Add an empty layer as described in step 4 on page 94. Then with the Art History Brush and **Wow-AH brush** chosen in step 2, **click on an area of contrast** to generate a series of brush strokes. Start with larger brushes and proceed to smaller ones until the canvas is filled with painted strokes.

*The painting was started with the **Wow-AH Oil-Large** Tool Preset (left) and then details were added with the **Medium** and **Small** versions (right).*

5 Enhance the painting. To improve color or texture, use any of the techniques described in step 5 starting on page 94.

*The oil painting after duplicating the paint layer, running the **Wow-Paint Edge Enhance-Subtle** Action, and applying the **Wow-Texture 01** Layer Style*

Brush Stroke Borders

*Quickly add a little personality to a photo using the **Wow-Art Media** Brush presets.*

▶ *The names of these Presets start with "BT," which stands for "Brush Tool," which is the tool you choose in the Tools palette in order to work with these Presets chosen from the Tool Presets palette.) Of course, these brushes can also be used for adding the finishing touches to a cloned painting as well.*

1 Enlarge the Canvas Visually. We'll need to add some extra space around our image in order to make room for a painted border. The added space will be filled with the current background color, so **press D** to set the background to white. Next, **press F** to enter full screen mode, **choose the Crop tool**, and **drag across the image**. After releasing the mouse button, **hold down the Option/Alt key and drag one of the corners beyond the image boundaries to the new desired size, and then press Enter.**

Expanding the Canvas size using the Crop tool

2 Load Presets and Paint. Before we can start painting, we'll need to load some tool presets by **choosing Window > Tool Presets** and then **choosing *Wow-Art Media Brushe*s** from the pop-out menu in the upper right of the palette (for more about loading presets, see page 3). Now choose the Brush tool, turn on the Current Tool Only checkbox at the bottom of the Tool Presets palette, and click on the **Wow-BT Oil-X Large** preset. Now that we're ready to paint, create a new layer by clicking the New Layer icon on the bottom of the Layers palette, change the foreground color to white, then paint around the edge of your image.

Selecting a Wow Art Media Preset

Painting with white on the newly created layer above our photograph Background

3 Add Layer Styles. We could complete this project at this point, but let's add a little "oomph" instead. Try applying your own Layer Style by **choosing Drop Shadow from the Layer Style pop-up menu** at the bottom of the Layers palette. In this case, set the opacity to 50 and the distance to zero, and adjust the size until you like the result (we used 30). This makes the details much more visible, thus creating a more elaborate edge effect. For a variation, try painting your frame with black and using an Outer Glow style to accentuate the details.

4. Apply Unsharp Mask Filter. Finally, to make the paint layer pop even more, **choose Filter > Sharpen > Unsharp Mask.** We used the following settings: Amount: 100, Radius: 1, Threshold: 0.

After you've gone through all the steps, you're welcome to turn off visibility for the current painted frame layer, create a new empty layer above it, and create another variation. Just click on a different tool preset and start painting. The examples below were created using the **Wow-BT Chalk-Large Chalk** and **Wow-BT Watercolor-Large** presets.

Applying a Drop Shadow to our Painted Frame layer

Painting with the Wow-BT Chalk-Large Chalk preset and...

... the Wow-BT Watercolor-Large preset

Painting Gallery

These "cloned" paintings were made using some of the **Wow-Pattern Stamp (PS)** and **Wow-Art History (AH)** presets shown on pages 100–101 and the methods described on pages 93–95. They were created at various sizes and Resolution settings and reduced to fit this layout.*

1 The strokes of the **PS Dry Brush** tools were enhanced with the **Texture 03** Style. **2 PS Chalk** with **Texture 07** creates the look of dry chalk on rough board. **3** This stylized illustration was converted to a painting using **PS Dry Brush** with **Texture 03**. **4 PS Watercolor** with **Texture 01** and **5 AH Oil** with **Texture 02** create two very different results from the same photo. **6 PS Watercolor**, with its Wet Edges and Airbrush settings, was used with **Texture 09** for a wet-into-wet effect. **7 AH Sponge** and **Texture 10** simulate paint dabbed onto stucco. **8 PS Watercolor** (with **Texture 01**) was used with smaller brush tips than in 4. **9** The automated strokes of the **AH Watercolor** tools, here with **Texture 01**, create a soft "wash" effect. **10** The pastel work was automated with **AH Chalk**, again with **Texture 01**. **11** Precise brush work for fine detail was created by using **PS Watercolor** and **Texture 01**.

1

2

3

4

5

Pattern Stamp & Art History Presets

These apple paintings were created from the photo below, using the **Wow-Pattern Stamp Brushes** and **Wow-Art History Brushes**, and were produced using a Wacom tablet. We utilized the five-step method outlined in "How To Paint with the Wow! Paint & Clone Presets" starting on page 93. The label under each picture identifies which Tool Preset and Texture Style (from pages 98–99) were used.

With the **Wow-Pattern Stamp (PS) Brushes**, you hand-paint each cloning stroke. The **Wow-Art History (AH) Brushes** are set up to apply strokes that automatically follow the contrast and color features of the source image. They clone much faster than the **PS** tools, but the automation means you have less creative control.

▶ *Here are ideas for using **Wow-PS Watercolor** Presets:*

- *To imitate a wash, use one continuous stroke rather than many short tones.*
- *Don't let colors touch or the details will blur.*
- *To add density to your watercolor, duplicate the painted layer (Ctrl/⌘-J) so the partially transparent colors build, and then adjust the Opacity of this top layer to taste.*

Wow-PS Watercolor + Texture 01

Wow-PS Oil + Texture 03

Wow-PS Dry Brush + Texture 02

Wow-PS Chalk + Texture 07

Wow-AH Watercolor + Texture 01

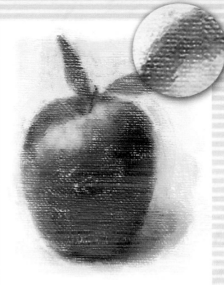

Wow-AH Oil + Texture 02

Wow-AH Pastel + Texture 01

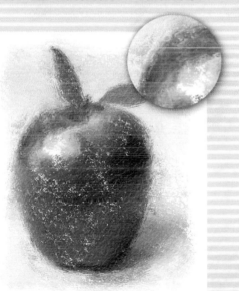

Wow-AH Chalk + Texture 07

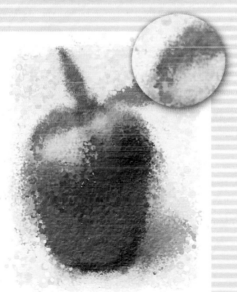

Wow-AH Stipple + Texture 10

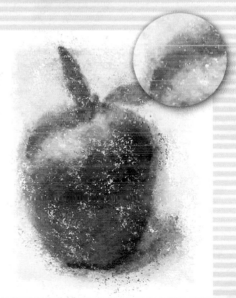

Wow-AH Sponge + Texture 09

Patterns Sampler

Adobe Photoshop CS2 One-Click Wow! also comes with a set of over 150 different seamlessly repeating Patterns, organized into seven different libraries. A random sampling of 36 of these different Patterns is shown on these two pages.

The categories of these different **Wow Patterns** include: **Fabric Patterns,** a collection of retro and tropical repeats; **Marble Patterns,** a series of polished tiles; **Media Patterns,** paper and canvas textures for backgrounds or overlays; **Noise Patterns,** especially good for mezzotint effects; **Organic Patterns,** a collection woven and handmade surfaces; and **Surface Patterns,** a set of abstracts and synthetic materials.

Wow Patterns can be used for a variety of effects. First, as a foundation for some layered collage project, create a Pattern Fill layer by selecting that option from the "Create a new fill or adjustment layer" icon/menu ⊘ at the bottom of the layer palette **A**, then select a general category of **Wow-Patterns** from the pop-out menus **B** and **C**, next select a specific one from the resulting list **B**. While this dialog box is open, move your cursor into the document window and click and drag to reposition the pattern.   *continued...*

| **Fabric 01** | **Fabric 02** | **Fabric 03** | **Fabric 04** | **Fabric 05** | **Fabric 06** |

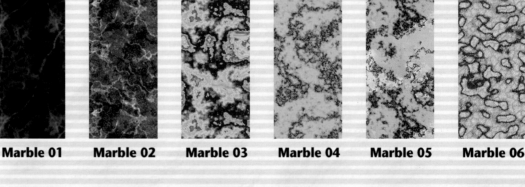

| **Marble 01** | **Marble 02** | **Marble 03** | **Marble 04** | **Marble 05** | **Marble 06** |

| **Media 01** | **Media 02** | **Media 03** | **Media 04** | **Media 05** | **Media 08** |

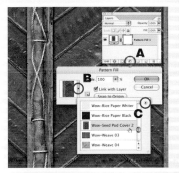

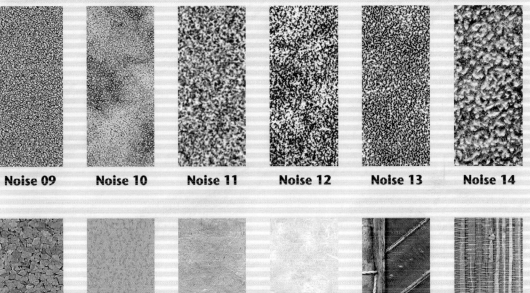

Noise 09 **Noise 10** **Noise 11** **Noise 12** **Noise 13** **Noise 14**

A second way to use a **Wow Pattern** is as an overlay. Many of the Wow Styles already have these custom patterns integrated in them, but by applying the patterns as a separate layer yourself, you will gain an additional level of control. To use a pattern as an overlay, first create a **Pattern Fill layer** above your background layer **D** as just described **E**, then simply change the Blending Mode **F** of the layer to Overlay (or have fun experimenting with other Blend Modes).

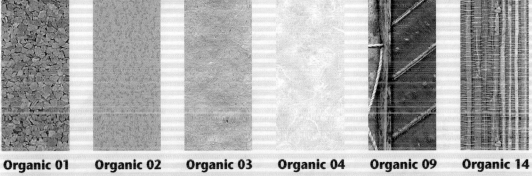

Organic 01 **Organic 02** **Organic 03** **Organic 04** **Organic 09** **Organic 14**

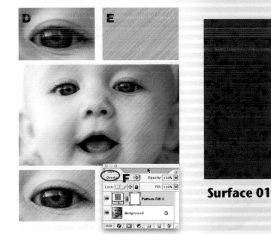

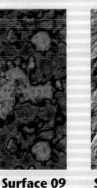

Surface 01 **Surface 02** **Surface 03** **Surface 05** **Surface 09** **Surface 26**

Using the Wow! Image Fix Brushes

Use these "fix-it" tools to tackle common problems.

▶ *Photoshop's new Healing Brush is useful for hiding blemishes and smoothing wrinkles. Here's an approach that does both, with a degree of subtlety that doesn't make skin look unnaturally smooth:*

1 *Duplicate the original photo to a new layer (Ctrl/⌘-J) and use the Healing Brush on anything you want to remove completely, such as blemishes, as described in the Photoshop User Guide.*

2 *Duplicate this "healed" layer (Ctrl/⌘-J), then use the Healing Brush again, this time to retouch the wrinkles. Then adjust the Opacity of this "wrinkles" layer to let some of the original "character lines" show through.*

The process of improving a photo should begin with overall tone and color adjustments and then proceed to retouching tasks. Here are some pointers for success:

1 Duplicate your image file (**choose File > Save As** and save under a new name). In case you make a mistake in your retouching, you'll have your original to go back to.

2 Next, make any necessary corrections to overall tone and color. You can try one of the **Wow-Image Fix Actions** to correct overall problems. If the result isn't quite what you want, in the Layers palette drag the Adjustment layer made by the Action to the trash can button at the bottom of the palette, then try a different **Wow-Image Fix Action**. 👁 *See "Using the Wow! Actions" on page 105 for directions.* Other subtle "quick fixes" you may try are **Wow-Darkroom Styles 11–15**; these are variations of **Wow-Darkroom 03**, which darkens the edges and lightens the center.

Try Wow-Darkroom Styles 11–15 to brighten an image. Step 4 on page 4 tells how to apply a Style.

3 Once you've made the overall corrections, you can go to work with the **Wow-Image Fix** brushes. With the **Wow-Tools** folder stored inside your Photoshop Tools folder (as described in step 1 on page 3), choose the Brush tool from Photoshop's Tools palette, then open the Tool Presets palette (**Window > Tool Presets**). Choose **Wow-Image Fix Brushes** from the palette's pop-out list, and use them as directed at the right.

To balance the lighting in an image, in the Tool Presets palette, choose a **Wow-Dodge&Burn** tool from the Tool Presets palette and paint with it, switching between black (to darken) and white (to lighten). Aim for subtle changes.

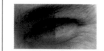

*Before (left) and after lightening with the **Wow-Dodge&Burn-Subtle** Preset, using white paint, a large soft brush tip, and low Opacity.*

If Photoshop CS2's **Red Eye Tool** doesn't give you preferable results, try the **Wow-Red Eye-Neutralize** brush at an appropriate size to carefully paint away the red in the pupil (and the iris if necessary). If you need to remove red from the iris, restore color with one of the three **Wow-Red Eye-Replace** brushes. If the pupil needs darkening, use the **Wow-Red Eye-Darken** brush.

*To correct red-eye, neutralize the red and restore color to the iris if necessary (center), and then darken the pupil if needed (right). You can use the bracket keys to change brush size— **[** to go smaller, **]** to enlarge.*

To whiten teeth or eyes, dab with an appropriate-size **Wow-White Teeth-Neutralize** brush to get rid of stains. (Stay away from lips and gums.) Then use the **Wow-White Teeth-Brighten** brush to lighten.

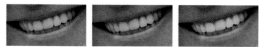

*Rather than aiming for a "Hollywood" smile, use the **Wow-White Teeth** brushes to neutralize specific stained areas (center), then whiten them (right).*

To take the "heat" out of red patches on the face but still leave some of the natural blush, use the **Wow-Red Skin-Neutralize** brush.

Using the Wow! Actions

These "try 'em, you'll like 'em" **Wow! Actions** *meet everyday Photoshop challenges and create some spectacular effects.*

▶ *Before you run any Action (Wow or not), make yourself a "safety net" by duplicating the file (choose Image > Duplicate). If you run the Action and don't like the result, close the "actioned" duplicate without saving it, go back to your original file, duplicate it again, and try a different Action. You can also use this safety net if a Stop message box appears as part of the Action and you decide you don't want to continue.*

▶ *With your Actions palette in list mode:*

- *Ctrl/⌘-clicking on an Action's name plays the Action.*
- *Double-clicking to the right of the name allows you to assign an F-key to the Action.*

There are five sets of Wow-Actions—"mini-programs" you can run in Photoshop for image fixing, dimensional effects for graphics, photo enhancements, enhancements for paintings, and production shortcuts.

1 Set up the Actions palette. Once you've copied the **Wow Actions** into the Photoshop Actions folder as described in step 1 on page 3, open the Actions palette (**choose Window > Actions**). By default the palette appears in List Mode, but you can toggle it to a compact and colorful set of buttons by choosing **Button Mode** from the menu that pops out from the palette's upper-right corner. Each **Wow-Actions** set that you choose from the bottom of that menu will be added to the palette.

2 Prepare the file. Open the file you want to run a Wow Action on, then make sure the image you want to start with is what's showing on-screen. That is, all the layers, masks, and Styles that make up the image must be visible. Also, target the layer you want the Action to work on (**click on the layer's name** in the Layers palette).

3 "Play" the Action. In the Actions palette, click the button for the Action you want to run. Basically, that's it—the Action runs!

Some of the Wow Actions start by making a duplicate file from whatever is visible in your image file. The Action then runs on that copy.

But if a Stop message box appears (it has a Stop button and often a Continue button also), be sure to read what it says and follow its instructions—it may tell you to make a selection, customize a setting, or adjust something to taste. If you don't do it, the Action won't work correctly.

Click the button to start the Action (above). It's important to read and carry out the directions in any "Stop" message. Then click the button again (it will be red, so you can find it) to continue.

Briefly, here are some examples of what the Wow Actions do:

Wow-Image Fix Actions. Among these is **Wow-Dust & Scratches Layer**, which helps you remove those tiny, annoying specks; it's faster than using Photoshop's Healing Brush, and you do the work on a separate layer, so you can't accidentally make your original worse. **Wow-Auto Levels Sampler** adds several Levels Adjustment layers for correcting common tone and color problems; after running the Action you can view the effect of each Adjustment layer and choose which works best. 👁 *See page 106 for more.*

Wow-Graphics Enhance Actions. These routines turn your active graphics or type layer into materials with characteristics like refraction or flame, which are too complex to achieve with a single Style.

Wow-Paint Enhance Actions. Try these after using the Wow painting and cloning Presets, to emphasize brush strokes or pooled paint.

Wow-Photo Enhance Actions. Try any of these 21 enhancements, such as watercolor, mezzotint, and framing, and see what happens.

Wow-Production Actions. These are shortcuts (especially in Button Mode) for everyday operations, like rotating a digital photo 90°.

Wow! Actions

You can accomplish the effects shown on these two pages (and more) by running the **Wow-Actions,** which are multistep automated "macros" that come in five sets. The examples on this page are from the **Wow-Graphics Enhance** Actions, and the examples on the facing page are from the **Wow-Photo Enhance** set, with the exception of one from the **Wow-Image Fix** set. (The starting graphic and photo are provided in the **Wow-Actions Testers** folder on the CD-ROM so you can experiment by running the **Wow-Actions** on them if you like.)

The **Wow Actions** are quick "try 'em, you'll like 'em" options. Some of them are as "instant" as Layer Styles. Others require that you interact with the Action as it runs. Follow the steps on page 105 to add these Actions to Photoshop's Actions palette, make a duplicate of your file, and finally, play an Action. **If a Stop message box appears, read and follow its instructions carefully —the Action needs your undivided attention at this point in order to get the correct results.**

Wow-Brushed Steel

Wow-Fire

Wow-Oiled Steel

Wow-Crystal   **Wow-Gold**   **Wow-Chrome**

*The **Wow Chrome and Crystal Actions** use your background photo for the reflection.*

Wow-Silver   **Wow-Distressed**

Wow-Brushed Metal

Wow-Dodge & Burn Layer
*From the **Wow-Image Fix** set;
before (right) and after (left)*

Wow-Color Background

Wow-Background Blur

Wow-Channel Mix-Pastels

Wow Filtered Watercolor

Wow Filtered Water+Line

Wow-Soft Focus-Lighten

Wow-Soft Focus-Overlay

Wow-Mezzotint-Gray

Wow-Linework Alone

Wow-Filtered Frame-Soft

Wow-Filtered Frame-Wood

Gradient Effects

The **Wow-Gradients** can be useful for filling type or graphics, or even for creating a background element. Three of the "rainbow" gradients (**04**, **05**, and **06**) create transparent top and bottom edges to allow part of the background to show through.

You can apply them with the **Gradient tool** or use them to create **Gradient Fill layers**, with all their customizable settings, such as gradient style, angle, and scale.

To create a Gradient Fill layer, click on the "Create a new fill or adjustment layer" icon at the bottom of the layer palette, then choose Gradient, then select the **Wow-Gradients** from the pop-out menus **A**, and select a specific one. While this dialog box is open, you can move your cursor into the document window and click and drag to reposition the gradient. Double click on the layer icon **B** at any time to change the settings.

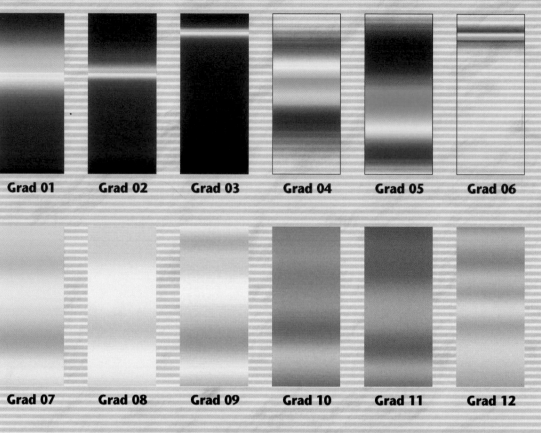

Grad 01   Grad 02   Grad 03   Grad 04   Grad 05   Grad 06

Grad 07   Grad 08   Grad 09   Grad 10   Grad 11   Grad 12

Grad 13   Grad 14   Grad 15   Grad 16   Grad 17   Grad 18

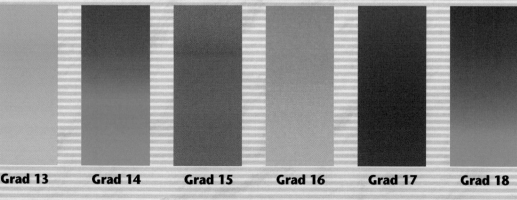

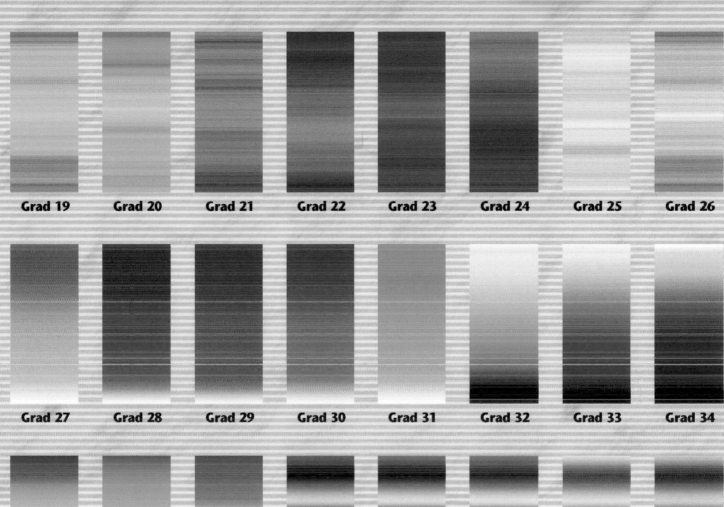

Grad 19	**Grad 20**	**Grad 21**	**Grad 22**	**Grad 23**	**Grad 24**	**Grad 25**	**Grad 26**
Grad 27	**Grad 28**	**Grad 29**	**Grad 30**	**Grad 31**	**Grad 32**	**Grad 33**	**Grad 34**

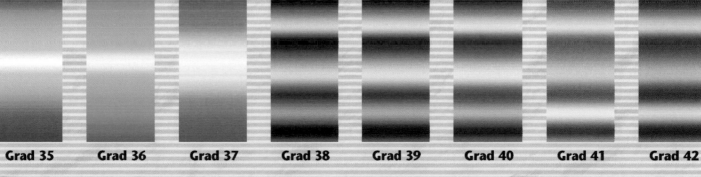

Grad 35	**Grad 36**	**Grad 37**	**Grad 38**	**Grad 39**	**Grad 40**	**Grad 41**	**Grad 42**

Notes

Notes

Notes

Notes

Notes